ENDEAVOUR

VOYAGE
OF THE
ENDEAVOUR

Captain Cook and the Discovery of the Pacific

ALAN FROST

ALLEN & UNWIN

First published in 1998 by
Allen & Unwin
9 Atchison Street,
St Leonards NSW 2065 Australia
Phone: (61 2) 9901 4088
Fax: (61 2) 9906 2218
E-mail: frontdesk@allen-unwin.com.au
Web: http://www.allen-unwin.com.au

National Library of Australia
Cataloguing-in-Publication entry:

Frost, Alan, 1943– .

The voyage of the Endeavour: Captain Cook and the discovery of the Pacific.

Includes index,
ISBN 1 86448 188 9.

1. Cook, James, 1728–1779—Journeys. 2. Pacific Ocean—Discovery and exploration. I. Title.

910.91

Set in 11.5/13.5 pt Goudy by DOCUPRO, Sydney
Printed by KHL, Singapore

10 9 8 7 6 5 4 3 2

Cover design: Steven Dunbar
Photograph of the Endeavour: John Longley
Engraved portrait of Cook: Mitchell Library, State Library of New South Wales
Internal design: Nada Backovic

CONTENTS

MAPS AND ILLUSTRATIONS

Maps

Illustrations

Boxed illustrations

PREFACE

As readers will quickly see, the records of the
early Pacific voyagers were not always perfectly
grammatical, and spelling in those days was a
rather haphazard affair. When quoting directly, I
have kept all the quirks of the originals. The only
changes I have made are to add clarifying details
in parentheses and to italicize the names of ships.

Understanding precise dates from the explorers' journals presents particular problems. English
navigators used to date time at sea from noon to
noon, i.e., 13 April 1770 ship's time went from
noon on 12 April to noon on 13 April. Cook
used ship's time in most of his journal of the
Endeavour's voyage, but switched to conventional
time while at Tahiti. On his second voyage,
thinking he might publish his journal, he kept
one version of it in conventional time. Moreover,

explorers often did not correct for crossing the 180° meridian of
longitude east or west of Greenwich (roughly today's International
Date Line), and thereby losing or gaining a day, until much later.
On his first voyage, for example, Cook, travelling west, did not add
a day for having crossed the meridian until he reached Batavia (now
Jakarta). Thinking that it would only add to the confusion to correct
them, I have kept all dates as the explorers gave them in their logs
and journals.

To make it easier for the reader to follow the story, I have usually
called countries by their modern names. Spain, for example, was
only emerging as a nation at the time of Columbus's voyage, and
the conquistadores who conquered Mexico, Peru and Chile certainly
did not know these regions by these names. However, I have used
them to avoid confusion.

For my general understanding of the European exploration of the Pacific Ocean in the second half of the eighteenth century, I owe a great debt to the many historians who have previously written on the subject, and an especially great debt to two in particular. Like everyone else who has written about the great ocean's history in the last 30 years, I have drawn very heavily on J.C. Beaglehole's monumental edition of Captain James Cook's journals (1955–1967). Thanks to their editor's meticulous scholarship and his very extensive annotations, the publication of these volumes began a new era in the study of European exploration and expansion, providing models for the editing of other explorers' journals.

I also owe a personal debt to Glyndwr Williams, Professor of History at Queen Mary and Westfield College, University of London. For almost twenty years now, whenever we have met—in England, Canada, or Australia—he and I have carried on an endless—and endlessly stimulating—discussion about exploration and culture contact, sharing our knowledge and pursuing new insights. I greatly value both this friendship and its intellectual exchange.

In places in this book, I present views that differ from those in the standard history books. Since this is a story for the general reader, I have not added notes setting out the evidence for these views, but I can assure readers that I have based them either on the most up-to-date scholarship or on extensive archival research. In a few years, I intend to publish a scholarly study of British imperialism in the second half of the eighteenth century, in which I shall document the basis of any unusual views.

It gives me much pleasure to think that this story will be available to those who come to look over the new *Endeavour* or sail on it. Today we see European imperialism in a very different light from our forebears. In particular, we know how devastating it often was to indigenous peoples and their cultures and environments. But I believe it is still possible both to acknowledge this devastation and, at the same time, to appreciate that the story of how Europeans explored the reaches of the globe is a great one. In the second half of the eighteenth century, this story was traced out in ships like the *Endeavour*. James Cook's story is inseparable from the story of the ships in which he sailed the Pacific. The *Endeavour* is the most famous of these, partly because it was the first, and partly because it sailed alone. Together, the stories of these eighteenth-century men and their vessels suggest the realities of all those who have gone down to the sea in ships, to do arduous business on the great waters.

INTRODUCTION

'This mysterious divine ocean,

this tide-beating heart of Earth'

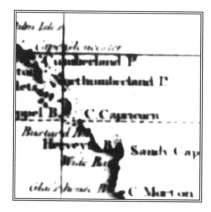

The expansion of Europe in modern times started in the early fifteenth century. After they captured Ceuta in North Africa from the Moors in 1415, seeking gold, spices and slaves, the Portuguese sent a series of expeditions out into the Atlantic Ocean and down the coast of Africa. By the 1450s, they had colonised the Canary Islands, Madeira and the Azores, and explored as far south as the Cape Verde Islands and Sierra Leone. In 1473, Portuguese navigators reached the equator, and by 1483 they were at the mouth of the Congo River. Five years later, in 1488, Bartolomeu Dias rounded the Cape of Good Hope, showing that there should be a sea route to the East.

By this time, Portugal's neighbour and rival Spain was also eager to explore the oceans. In 1492, sailing in the service of King Ferdinand and Queen Isabella of Castile, and seeking an east-to-west route to China, Christopher Columbus crossed the Atlantic Ocean and reached the islands of the Caribbean. It was not until his third voyage, in 1498, that Columbus realised that not far beyond these islands lay a continent (though he continued to believe this was Asia rather than a new discovery). In the same year, the Portuguese Vasco da Gama pioneered a west-to-east route around southern Africa. Sailing from Lisbon with five ships in July 1497, Gama reached Calicut on the western side of India in May 1498, and returned a year later with a cargo of spices, woods and jewels.

By this time, the Catholic nations Portugal and Spain had divided the non-European world between them. Believing that his title gave him the right to dispose of islands not in Christian possession, in 1493 the Pope issued two edicts, or bulls, making Spain and Portugal the overlords of the newly discovered lands. The next year, by the Treaty of Tordesillas, the two nations formally partitioned the globe. Drawing a longitudinal line on the map 370 leagues (about 2200 km) west of the Cape Verde Islands (roughly in the middle of the Atlantic Ocean), they agreed that Spain would have all islands lying to the west of the line and Portugal all islands to the east.

In the next twenty years, both nations continued their expansion. In 1500, the Portuguese commander Pedro de Cabral took thirteen ships out to India, discovering Brazil on the way. Portuguese expeditions reached Ceylon in 1506, Malacca in 1511, and the Banda Islands, Amboina and the Moluccas (Spice Islands) the next year. In the western hemisphere, the Spanish established settlements on West Indian islands and made forays onto what they now knew to be the mainland (*Tierra Firme*).

It was during one of these probes that a European first saw the vast expanse of water that a later voyager, Herman Melville, was to term 'this mysterious divine [ocean], [this] tide-beating heart of earth'. Crossing the Isthmus of Panama from the north, on or about 25 September 1513, from the height of the dividing range Vasco Nuñez de Balboa saw an ocean spreading limitlessly southwards to the curved horizon. On 29 September, holding forth a banner, he strode into the water and claimed the 'South' Sea and all its islands for Spain.

These discoveries raised the question of where the Tordesillas line, if it were continued through the Poles, would bisect the eastern hemisphere, and particularly whether the coveted Spice Islands lay in Spain's or Portugal's part of the globe. The resolution of these questions was bedevilled by false assumptions about the circumference of the globe and, accordingly, about the extent of a degree. Columbus had sailed thinking that a degree was one-quarter less in distance than it actually is, and that the ocean lying between western Europe and China (since he was unaware America existed) extended through only 68°. That is, he believed it was only about 4400 km from the Canaries to Japan, whereas in reality it is about 20 000 km.

Since Spanish navigators were forbidden to sail to the East through Portugal's hemisphere, they might only reach the Spice and other islands at the western fringe of Spain's hemisphere by finding an alternative route through or around the Americas. In September 1519, Ferdinand Magellan, a Portuguese who had served in the East but who had fallen from favour at home, sailed for the rulers of Castile in search of such a route. Coasting southwards along South America, Magellan passed through the straits that bear his name in November 1520, crossed the ocean in a northwesterly direction, and reached the Philippine Islands in March 1521. He was killed in fighting in Cebu, but some of his crew completed the voyage—the first circumnavigation of the globe. The trip was a terrible one. Between South America and Guam, the seamen sighted only a handful of insignificant islands; and scurvy (see box pp. 86–7) wreaked terrible havoc. One of the voyagers, Antonio Pigafetta, wrote:

> we stayed [at sea] three months and twenty days without taking on victuals or other refreshments, and we ate only old biscuit turned to powder all full of worms and stinking with the odour of the urine the rats had made on it, after eating the good part. And we drank putrid yellow water. We also ate the hides of cattle which were very hard because of the sun, rain, and wind. And we left them four or five days in the sea, then put them for a little while over the coals. And so we ate them. Also rats which cost half a crown each one. And even so we could not find enough of them.

Yet Magellan and his men encountered no storms as they crossed the ocean, so they named it the Pacific. With this voyage, for the first time Europeans began to comprehend the immensity of this expanse of water, which covers one-third of the globe.

Competition for colonies and trade

Spain and Portugal continued expanding their empires throughout the sixteenth century. By 1514 the Portuguese had reached southern China and by 1543, Japan. After that, they consolidated their bridgeheads in Africa and Asia, and set up an extensive trading network around the Indian Ocean. They also began colonising Brazil. In the western hemisphere, Spain continued its colonisation of the West Indian islands and the Isthmus of Panama, and conquered the Aztec empire in Mexico (1519–21) and the Inca empire in Peru (1530–33). The Spanish began to occupy Chile in the early 1540s and Argentina from the 1580s onwards.

But the Iberian nations did not have the new worlds to themselves for long. Envious of the wealth and power their southern rivals had obtained, the northern European powers started moving in on the West Indies in the mid-sixteenth century. In the 1530s, French privateers harassed Spanish shipping and towns, to be followed by English 'sea dogs' from the 1560s, and Dutch towards the turn of the seventeenth century. In the last decades of the sixteenth century and the first of the seventeenth century, too, came attempts at settlement. The English established control over Newfoundland in 1583; and failed ventures in Virginia in the 1580s were succeeded by a more enduring one there from 1607. Religious separatists began to colonise New England in 1620. Having started a fur trade in Canada in the 1560s, the French began settling Nova Scotia in 1605 and Quebec in 1608. The Dutch began to colonise New York in 1626.

In the Caribbean, after Walter Raleigh's abortive attempts to colonise Guyana in the 1590s, there was a British settlement on St Kitts in 1625, and another on Barbados in 1627. The French also settled St Kitts in 1625, and Martinique and Guadeloupe in the mid-1630s. Early in the seventeenth century, the Dutch too took up the pursuit of territory, occupying Essequibo in 1616. With the aid of their own West India Company, formed in 1621, they went on to settle Berbice in 1624, and Curaçao in 1635. Between 1630 and 1650, the Dutch also controlled a large area of northern Brazil. Later in the century, as Spanish power waned and European demand for tobacco, sugar and rum rose, these northern nations extended their colonies (though the Portuguese expelled the Dutch from northern Brazil).

Though it happened later, the story in Portugal's hemisphere was much the same. The Dutch reached the East Indies in the 1590s, and in the following years established trading posts (known as factories) in Bantam, Acheen, Amboina and other places, and in Japan. Within 30 years, they had made Batavia (Jakarta) their headquarters, set up an administrative system to regulate spice production and centralise trade in the archipelago, and all but expelled the English. By the middle of the century, they had greatly diminished the Portuguese presence in the East Indies and in Ceylon. By its end, they had a territorial empire with which to underwrite their trading one. As they established themselves in the East Indies, they also set up factories on the coasts of India. After capturing Negapatam on the southeast coast from the Portuguese in 1658, they made it their principal base there. Although the Dutch were unable to become the biggest power in India, they remained masters of the East Indies until the mid-1790s, and were the chief suppliers of the spices—pepper, cinnamon, nutmeg, cloves—which Europeans so craved.

The English moved into the East at the same time as the Dutch. Queen Elizabeth I granted a royal charter to the Governor and Company of Merchants of London trading into the East Indies at the end of 1600, and after the Dutch had forced them from the archipelago they shifted their ventures to India, where, throughout the seventeenth century, they developed a profitable trade in indigo, cotton goods, saltpetre, pepper, cinnamon, sugar, calicoes, and coffee. By the century's end, they had opened a trade with China. After this company was reorganised at the beginning of the eighteenth century, the merchants steadily strengthened their position. By 1750, they had divided their now substantial Indian holdings into three 'presidencies' centred on Bombay, Fort St George (Madras) and Fort William (Calcutta); and they maintained satellite factories at surrounding points.

Though the French also became interested in overseas colonies and trade at the beginning of the seventeenth century, they did nothing substantial in the East until 1664, when King Louis XIV granted a charter to the Compagnie des Indes Orientales. This company established factories at various points in India, but did not prosper much in 50 years, and soon after it was incorporated into the Compagnie des Indes in 1719, the combine went bankrupt. But some French traders continued to operate in the East. By the mid-eighteenth century they had developed a large factory at Pondicherry, and smaller ones at Mahe, Calicut, Surat, Masulipatam, and Chandernagore.

The rise of European navies

Since the potential rewards of defeating a rival nation in war were more alluring than ever, by the eighteenth century the European nations were going to war more and more often. To protect their far-flung possessions (and attack their rivals') they had to develop powerful navies that could be deployed anywhere about the globe. The British, for example, started enlarging the role of the Royal Navy during the War of the Spanish Succession (1702–13). Thanks to their capture of Gibraltar (1704) and Minorca (1708), they were able to deploy a squadron permanently in the Mediterranean. In the 1720s and 1730s, Port Royal, Jamaica, and English Harbour, Antigua, became the bases of the British West India squadrons. At the start of the War of Jenkins's Ear (1739–48), Rear Admiral Edward Vernon was sent with a squadron to ravage Spain's Caribbean settlements, and Lord Anson set off with another to attack its settlements and ships on the west coasts of the Americas. After the Jacobites (supporters of Bonnie Prince Charlie) were defeated in 1745, the British established a permanent squadron in North America. Also, from 1745 to 1749 they kept a squadron in the East Indies, based in Trincomalee in Dutch Ceylon. In the Seven Years War (1756–63), the British fought the French in North America, the West Indies, and India; and they attacked Manila as well as Havana. After the war, they retained a small squadron in Indian waters, and in the American Revolutionary wars of 1776–83, there were extensive naval operations there, in addition to those off northern Europe, in the Mediterranean, off North America and Africa and in the West Indies.

Daniel Baugh has identified the general nature of this expansion well:

The growth of the British navy in the eighteenth century was to a large extent the direct result of its radically enlarged strategic commitments in foreign waters. Between 1689 and 1714 England assumed a role in continental conflicts which, whether she liked it or not, she could not renounce, and as a natural consequence of this role the Mediterranean turned into a major theater of operations for the British navy. Simultaneously colonies and foreign trade prospered, and Whig governments were neither able nor inclined to deny colonists and merchants the protection they demanded from piracy, privateering, and the raids of plunder. Moreover, naval strenth had to be found, not only to defend the empire, but also to support a policy of expanding its boundaries by conquest. All of these things had been necessary at one time or another before. But where a cruiser had sufficed in the seventeenth century, it was now often necessary to employ a squadron; what had been a squadron's task now seemed impossible without a fleet; and what had been accomplished by an expedition now required a permanently stationed force.

The same could be said of the French and Spanish navies in the period.

But it wasn't only navies that grew as a result of war. Paradoxical as it may at first seem, during each period of conflict, the British merchant marine also increased in size. For example, in 1702 there were approximately 323 000 tons burden of English-owned shipping. In 1756, there were 468 000 tons; in 1774 there were 588 000 tons; and in 1786 there were 752 000 tons. Again, in 1748 there were approximately 150 000 tons burden of shipping employed in the North American, West Indian and East Indian trades, whereas by 1775 there were 300 000 tons. The French and Spanish merchant marines grew along similar lines. The huge increase in the number of ships, and in the activities they supported, led to the European powers incorporating much of the non-European world into their economic and political systems. The increase also meant that, by the end of the century, these powers were experiencing severe shortages in ship's timber and other naval materials.

Gold and buccaneers

Until the mid-eighteenth century, the Pacific Ocean was the scene of comparatively little of this vast commercial and imperial expansion. After several unsuccessful attempts in the 1520s to gain a foothold in the Moluccas (which failed partly because of the sheer difficulty of returning to Mexico by a route close to the equator), Spain switched its attention to the Philippine Islands, establishing a settlement on Cebu in 1565 and another at Manila four years later. This colonization also led to the discovery of a viable return route from Asia, along an arc high in the north Pacific then down the northwest American coast to Acapulco. The Spanish later developed an extended system of trade with Asia. Every year they sent from Acapulco to Manila galleons loaded with gold and silver from the mines of Mexico and Peru. At Manila, the bullion was exchanged for goods from China and other countries, such as silks, porcelains and medicines. These were then taken back to Mexico, transported overland to Vera Cruz, and transshipped to Seville.

For 250 years, the great Manila galleons crossed and recrossed the northern Pacific Ocean. With favourable following winds, the voyage from Acapulco to Manila usually took about three months. That in the other direction was much more difficult. Taking five to seven months (or longer), and with no place of refreshment midway, it could, one survivor wrote, 'be called the longest and most horrible passage in the world . . . because of the terrible storms that are met with one after another, and because of the grave illnesses that carry men off'.

In addition to venturing north of the equator to the East Indian and Philippine islands, the Spanish also made a number of probes

Spanish voyages in the Pacific Ocean in the Sixteenth Century: The Northern Voyages of

to the south of the equator. With biblical notions of King Solomon's mines, and having heard Inca stories of voyages to islands to the west from which men returned with gold, slaves and the skins of horse-like animals, Alvaro de Mendaña sailed from Callao on the coast of Peru in 1567, and in February the next year reached the large Melanesian islands he named the Solomons. Thirty years later,

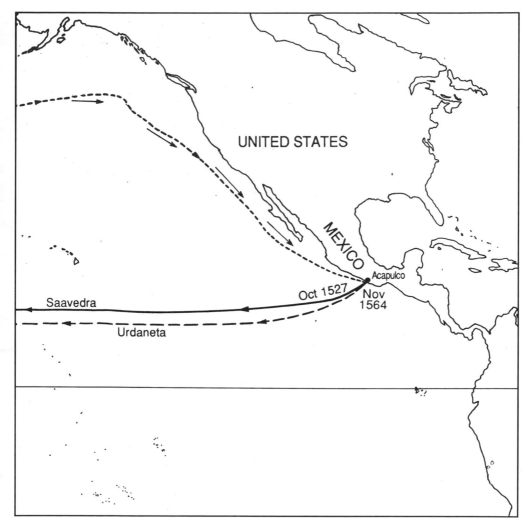

Saavedra 1527–8 and Urdaneta 1564–5.

in 1595, Mendaña led a second expediton, with Pedro Fernández de Quirós as pilot. They found the Marquesas Islands, then the Santa Cruz archipelago, before Mendaña's death and other problems forced his subordinates to abandon the venture.

Believing that they had in fact found the fringe of the reputed Great Southern Continent, Quirós tried again in 1605, with Luis

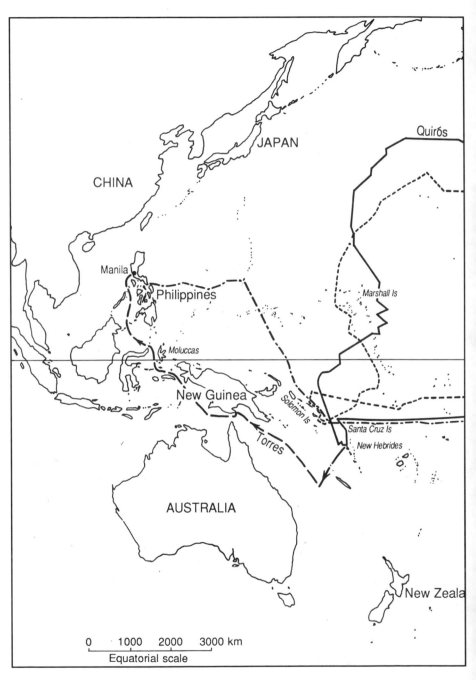

Spanish Voyages in the Pacific Ocean in the Sixteenth and Early Seventeenth Centuries:

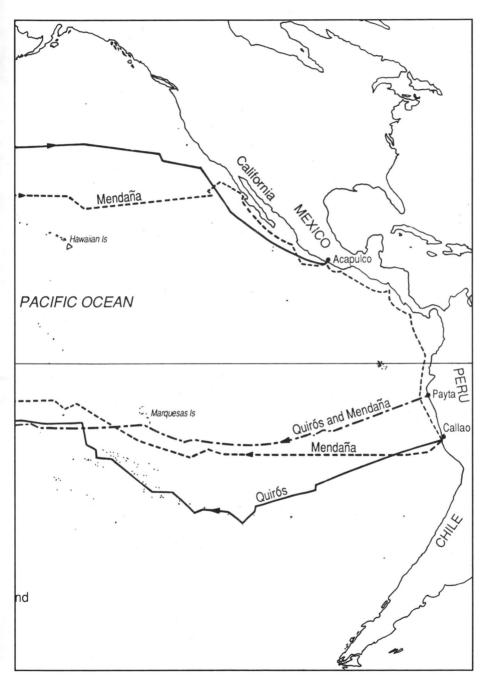

The Southern Voyages of Mendaña 1567–8, Mendaña and Quirós 1595, and Quirós and Torres 1605–6.

Váez de Torres as his deputy. In April 1606, they found the island group later known as the New Hebrides (now Vanuatu), and Quirós set about founding his dreamt-of colony. Then, mysteriously, he suddenly sailed off, to reach the coast of California in October. Torres took the rest of the party to Manila through the strait that bears his name.

The other European maritime nations did not venture very much into the Pacific Ocean. The Portuguese seem to have made a few tentative voyages east from Malacca in the 1520s, but where to remains a mystery. The Parmentier brothers, sailing out of the northern French port of Dieppe, *may* have reached the western Pacific in about 1528, but again this is unclear. After becoming famous for raiding a silver-laden mule train in Panama, in 1577–80 Francis Drake circumnavigated the globe, on the way capturing an Acapulco treasure galleon and sojourning on the west coast of North America somewhere near San Francisco. In the seventeenth century, the Portuguese, Spanish and English lost their tentative trade to Japan to the Dutch, who from 1641 were allowed to maintain a single factory on an island in Nagasaki harbour. In the seventeenth and early eighteenth centuries, countless buccaneers tried to emulate Drake's raid, among them Henry Morgan, who sacked Panama City in 1671; William Dampier, who participated in the sacking of towns and the capture of ships on the Pacific coasts of Spain's colonies from the 1670s into the eighteenth century; and Woodes Rogers, who captured a galleon from Manila on 1 January 1710. Also at the beginning of the eighteenth century (1701–17), when Spain's imperial control was relaxed, about 170 French merchantmen sailed to the towns on the west coast of South America, where they traded.

But between 1600 and 1750, there were few genuine exploring voyages in the Pacific. I have already mentioned that of Quirós and Torres in 1605–06. In 1615, seeking to avoid the Dutch East India Company's monopoly, Jacob Le Maire and Willem Schouten sailed south around Cape Horn. After finding the island of Juan Fernández, and seeking unsuccessfully for Quirós's supposed *Terra Australis*, they went north of New Guinea to the East Indies, where the governor-general seized their ship and sent them home. Dutch authorities in the East Indies themselves mounted a number of voyages of exploration between 1606 and 1644, including those of Abel Tasman, first in 1639, in search of the Islands of Silver and Gold thought to lie east of Japan; and then in 1642–43, east past Tasmania to New Zealand and up the western Pacific. Sir John Narborough led a British Admiralty expedition up the west coast of South America in 1670 which was intended both to explore and to establish trading links. Bringing back much new information about the coasts of southern America, he succeeded quite well at the first task, but failed miserably at the second. In 1698, William Dampier was given command of the *Roebuck* for a voyage to Australia and the Pacific, during which he went north of New Guinea and showed that it was separate from New Britain. In 1721–22, Jacob Roggeveen led an expedition on behalf of the Dutch West India Company. Rounding Cape Horn, he discovered Easter Island, then sailed through the northern Tuamotus and past Samoa, and rounded New Guinea to the East Indies.

The tyranny of winds

One reason for the comparative lack of imperial activity in the Pacific Ocean was that, of all the European nations, only Spain had settlements in it or around its rim—and settlements were essential to support extended voyages. So long as the other powers could not see convincing reasons to commit the money and resources needed to establish settlements of their own, they remained at a clear disadvantage. Only quick returns, such as from sacking towns, capturing treasure ships, or trading with the local populations at times when imperial authority was lax, justified the enormous expenses and risks involved in voyages round South America—and these returns were usually only available in times of war.

But there was another reason, too. The wind and current systems in both halves of the great ocean militated against navigators sailing outside the areas known by the end of the fifteenth century. In the southern hemisphere, the westerly winds and currents sweep underneath Australia, past New Zealand and across the Pacific until they

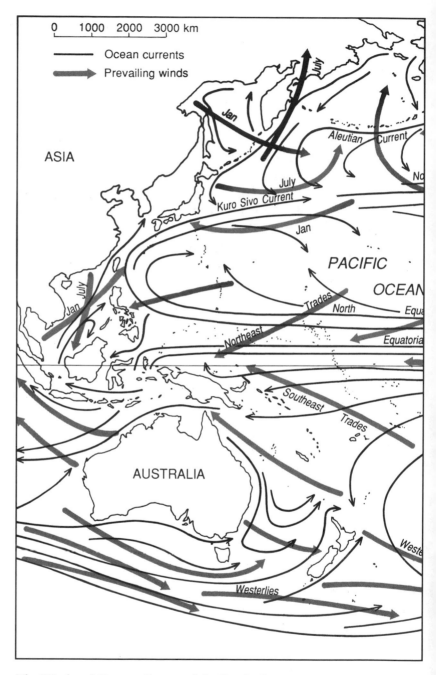

The Wind and Current System of the Pacific Ocean.

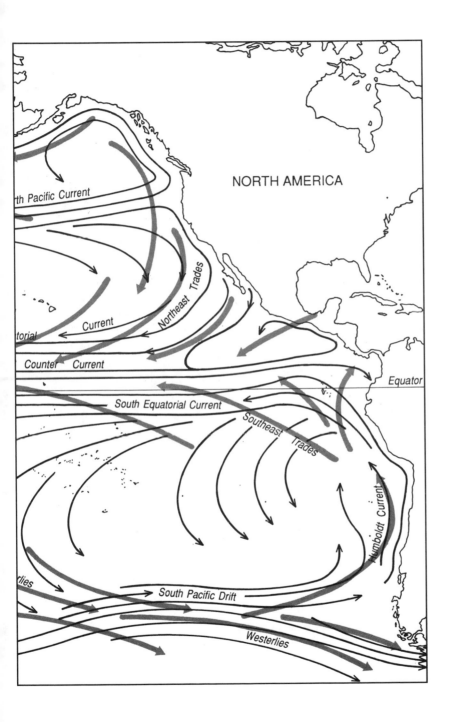

reach South America. There they divide, with one branch running up the coast until it turns west beneath the equator. Navigators of sailing ships entering the Pacific from the east, either through the Straits of Magellan or round Cape Horn, had no choice but to turn north until they caught the southeast trade wind at their back somewhere near the Tropic of Capricorn, and then to take a westerly course. With the winds and currents just to the north of the equator also running east to west, and given the screen of islands and coral reefs to the south and east of New Guinea, it was also inevitable that navigators would go north round this massive island to reach the ports of the Philippines or the East Indies. With the exception of Torres in 1606, this was the general route of all east-to-west crossings of the Pacific until James Cook's first voyage.

In the northern hemisphere, while the wind and current systems easily carried ships above the equator up to the Ladrones and then among the Philippines, they also made it impossible to return to America along the same route. Not until Andres de Urdaneta took a wide sweep north from the Philippines in 1565 did the Spanish find a viable return route, and even then they took it at great risk.

To explore further in the Pacific Ocean, and to extend commercial systems throughout it, required new outlooks, new technologies, and new reasons for venturing. These things emerged together in the mid-eighteenth century, and gave rise to the greatest period of deliberate exploration in human history. It is the story of this exploration which I shall now tell.

1

WAR, DISCOVERY AND TRADE

Exploring the Pacific, 1748–1766

At the end of June 1764, two Royal Navy ships exhibiting the new technique of copper sheathing, the 24-gun frigate *Dolphin* and the sloop *Tamar*, sailed down the English Channel and south into the Atlantic Ocean. The official story was that these ships were bound for India to reinforce the small squadron there and deliver Captain John Byron to be its commodore. This pretence was sustained well past the departure date. On 18 June, three days before the ships left Plymouth, the East India Company asked if they would carry some despatches for it. And in October, when Robert Clive, returning to Bengal on one of the last Company ships of the season, reached Rio de Janeiro to find the *Dolphin* and *Tamar*, which 'left England a month after us, and anchored here nearly a month before us', he  lamented what he saw as a lost opportunity, writing home to the prime minister: 'Had the situation of affairs permitted you, Sir, to suggest to me the Commodore's destination, it would certainly have saved me much time; however, I propose embarking upon the *Dolphin* at the Cape of Good Hope, which will shorten my passage six weeks or two months.' The new governor-general of the East India Company's settlements in the East must have been disappointed again when he reached Cape Town, for the *Dolphin* and *Tamar* had not been bound for India at all, but for the southern Atlantic and Pacific Oceans, in search of undiscovered continents and islands and the supposed passage across North America linking the Atlantic and the Pacific.

Until recently, the origins of Byron's voyage were mysterious. Presumably, the decision to mount it was made quite consciously by the Lords Commissioners of the Admiralty, and probably also by cabinet ministers, yet no memoranda proposing it and explaining its purposes seem to exist. However, recent research indicates that Byron's voyage was not a new scheme but the revival of one put forward sixteen years earlier.

In 1740–44, during the war with Spain, George Anson had led a naval expedition into the Pacific Ocean to attack Spanish settlements and shipping on the west coasts of the Americas, and, if possible, to establish links with the Creole and Indian populations which might lead to commercial connections. The expedition proved a harrowing one. Setting out with six ships and 1955 men, Anson ended the voyage with only one ship and 145 of his original men. More than 1300 of his crews had died, the vast majority of them from scurvy. However, Anson did succeed in capturing a galleon sailing from Mexico to the Philippines laden with silver, and returned to England a hero.

Between 1744 and 1748, Dr John Campbell published a revised edition of John Harris's *Navigantium atque Itinerantium Bibliotheca* (Library of Voyages and Travels). Like many of his countrymen, Campbell was awestruck by Anson's feats; and he discoursed at length on 'the great Importance of new Discoveries, and the Advantages which a trading Nation may derive from the opening fresh Channels of Communication with the inhabitants of distant Countries, and consequently of disposing of their Commodities and Manufactures, in Places, where, perhaps, they were never seen or heard of before'. In particular, he urged that efforts be made to discover the supposed Northwest Passage from the Atlantic to the Pacific:

> *if ever a Passage could be this Way found . . . we might, very probably, reach, in six Weeks, Countries that we cannot now visit in twelve or fifteen Months; and this by an easy and wholesome Navigation, instead of those dangerous and sickly Voyages, that have hitherto rendered the Passage into the South Seas a thing so infrequent and ingrateful to British Seamen. If such a Passage could be found, it would bring us upon the unknown [i.e., west] Coasts of North America; which we have*

*many good Reasons to believe are very populous, inhabited by a
rich and civilized People, no Strangers to Trade, and with whom
we might carry on a very great and beneficial Commerce.*

There was also the discovery of New Holland and New Guinea to
be completed, with perhaps a colonisation of New Britain, from which
'a great Trade might be carried on from thence through the whole
Terra Australis on one Side, and the most valuable Islands of the *East
Indies* on the other'. Perhaps, too, an intermediate settlement should
be made on Juan Fernández, and another on 'the most Southern Part
of *Terra Australis*', so as to take advantage of the 'Product and
Commodities' of the southland, which must be 'extremely rich and
valuable', 'because the richest and finest Countries in the known world
lie all of them within the same Latitude' (i.e. 0°–44°).

These views accorded closely with those advanced by Richard
Walter and Benjamin Robins in the account of Anson's circumnavigation which they published in 1748. While his name is nowhere
given as the author, it is clear that their views on strategy and trade
are in fact Anson's, arrived at after much reflection on the lessons
of his voyage, and on how best the purposes of war against or
commerce with Spain's American colonies might in future be promoted. In the famous ninth chapter of Book I, 'Observations and
directions for facilitating the passage of our future Cruisers round
Cape Horn', Anson urged, first, that Britain colonise the Falkland
Islands so as to create a way station on the route around the south
of America where ships could refresh: 'this might open to us facilities
of passing into the *Pacifick* Ocean, which as yet we may be unacquainted with, and would render all the southern navigation
infinitely securer than at present.' Second, he pointed to the island
of Juan Fernández as 'the properest port for cruisers to refresh at on
their first arrival in the *South-Seas*', and as the base from which such
ships might patrol across established shipping routes. Together, he
thought, possession of these locations would enable Britain to
control the navigation of the southeastern Pacific: 'I doubt not but
a voyage might be made from *Falkland*'s Isles to *Juan Fernandes* and
back again, in little more than two months. This, even in time of

peace, might be of great consequence to this Nation; and, in time of war, would make us masters of those seas.' Like Campbell, Anson argued for a program of deliberate exploration to realise these goals:

> *by whatever means navigation is promoted, the conveniences hence arising must ultimately redound to the emolument of Great-Britain. Since as our fleets are at present superior to those of the whole world united, it must be a matchless degree of supineness or mean-spiritedness, if we permitted any of the advantages which new discoveries, or a more extended navigation may produce to mankind, to be ravished from us.*

We now know that Anson not only publicised these views but also persuaded the British government to pursue them. On 19 January 1749, at the Admiralty, 'Lord Anson signified his Majesty's Pleasure that Two Sloops should be forthwith fitted to be sent on Discoverys in the Southern Latitude.' The Navy then proceeded to fit out the *Porcupine* and *Raven* for this expedition, until Spain objected strenuously. This led Lord Sandwich, the head of the Admiralty, to explain the purposes of the voyage in detail:

> *[The ships are to] proceed to the Coast of Brasil to wood & Water, & from thence go in Search of Peppys Island which is supposed to be to the Eastward of Cape Blanco, from thence to go to Falkland's Islands, & after having made what Discoveries they can in those Parts, to return to Brasil to clean & refit for the farther intended discovery, on which they are to set forward in the proper Season. They are then to double Cape Horn, & to water at Juan Fernandez, from thence to proceed into the Trade Winds keeping between the Latitudes of 25° & 10° Sth & to steer a traverse Course for at least 1000 leagues [c. 5900 kilometres] or more if they have an opportunity of recruiting their Wood & Water; after which they are to haul*

*into the variable Winds way, & return back by Cape Horn to
the Coast of Brasil.*

One of the reasons for this plan to explore the southern Pacific
Ocean was the belief that it held a great continent such as the one
depicted by Ortelius on his world map of 1570 and by a host of
mapmakers since. Another likely reason was a story relayed to British
authorities by Henry Hutchinson, who had lived for many years in
Spanish America and been agent-victualler to Anson's expedition.
He had heard that there were 'some Good Islands' to the west of
Peru, 'which had been seen, and are often talkd of by the Spaniards
. . . who say, through Policy, those Islands have not been sought
after in a proper manner . . . owing to the fear of their being
discover'd by other Nations'.

Even though Sandwich offered to cancel the second part of
Porcupine and *Raven's* expedition, the Spanish remained deeply suspicious. They believed that the papal bulls of 1493 and the Treaty of
Tordesillas of 1494, whereby Spain and Portugal had divided the
non-European world between them, had given them 'an exclusive right'
to navigate in the southern Atlantic and Pacific Oceans, and to possess
colonies in most of South America; and that the other European
nations had implicitly recognised this right in the Treaty of Utrecht
(1713). Second, the Spanish too had read the account of Anson's
voyage, and saw only too well what the implications of a British
presence in the southern oceans around America would be. As Spanish
Foreign Minister Don José de Carvajal told the British ambassador at
Madrid, Pepys and Falklands Islands 'had been long since first discovered and inhabited by the Spaniards, who called them Islands de Leones
from the Quantities of these Amphibious Animals to be met with upon
their Coasts'. If the British did not intend to follow exploration with
settlement, what use would the discovery be, Carvajal asked pointedly.
He hoped, reported the ambassador, that the British

*would consider what Air it would have in the World to see us
[the British] planted directly against the Mouth of the*

*Streights of Magellan, ready upon all Occasions to enter into
the South Seas, where the next Step would be to endeavour to
discover and settle in some other Islands, in order to remedy the
Inconveniency of being obliged to make so long a Voyage
as that to China, to refit our Naval Force upon any
Disappointment we might meet with in our future Attacks
upon the Spanish Coasts, as had happened to My Lord Anson.*

The British replied that they wanted to explore only 'for the Advancement of Knowledge', but the Spanish remained bitterly opposed to the scheme.

In the interests of international harmony, the British agreed to 'lay [the scheme of discovery] aside *for the present*'. In doing so, however, they reserved the right to take up again at some future time 'this Plan for discovery of New Countries & Islands in the American Seas', cautioning that 'his Majesty cannot in any respect give into the reasonings of the Spanish Ministers, as his Right to send Ships for the discovery of unknown & unsettled Parts of the World, must indubitably be allowed by every body'. In his final dispatch home on the subject, the British ambassador wrote: 'If after all Our attentions these People should be stubborn & resty, I should be the first to advise a contrary behaviour, and if they would vex us, We have matters & ways to vex them in Our turn without infringing our Treaties, & one of my first steps should be the setting out upon discoveries in the South Seas.' So although in 1749 the British decided not to take up Anson's scheme for exploring in the southern Atlantic and Pacific Oceans, they did not abandon the idea that they might do so at some future time.

'Lands and islands of great extent'

That time did not arrive until after the end of the Seven Years War (1756–63), in which Britain established a clear naval dominance over its arch rivals France and Spain. This time, the British authorities, led by the Earl of Egmont, the new First Lord Commissioner of the Admiralty, took care to avoid the opposition to Pacific exploration encountered in 1749 by planning the voyage in great secrecy and banning foreigners from the dockyards where the ships were being fitted out. They gave command of the expedition to Captain John Byron, who had been a junior officer on Anson's expedition but had been shipwrecked on the coast of Chile and made a slow and painful way back to England. The core of the Admiralty's secret instructions to Byron read:

Whereas there is reason to believe that Lands and Islands of great extent hitherto unvisited by any European Power may be found in the Atlantick Ocean between the Cape of Good Hope and the Magellanick Streight, within Latitudes convenient for Navigation, as likewise His Majesty's Islands called Falkland's Islands, lying within the said Tract, notwithstanding the first discovery and possession thereof taken by Cowley in 1686, and notwithstanding the visitation thereof by Dampier and other British navigators, have never yet been so sufficiently surveyed, as that an accurate judgement may be formed of their Coasts or Product; And more over as the Countrey of New Albion [California] in North America first discovered and taken possession of by Sir Francis Drake in the Year 1579, has never been examined with that care which it deserves, notwithstanding frequent recommendations of that Undertaking by the said Sir Frans. Drake, Dampier, & many other Mariners of great Experience, who have thought it probable that a passage might be found between the Latitude of 38° and 54° from that Coast into Hudson's Bay . . .

Byron was first to search the south Atlantic for 'Land or Islands'. If he found any, he was 'to make purchases, with the consent of [the] Inhabitants, and take possession of convenient Situations in the Country, in the Name of the King of Great Britain'; or if the

❧ NAVIGATION ❧

Although the early Pacific voyagers had the compass to tell them which direction they were headed in, they often had trouble working out their exact position. To do this, they needed two measurements: latitude (distance north or south of a fixed point, usually the equator) and longitude (distance east or west of a fixed point, conventionally the Greenwich meridian, 0°).

Determining latitude was relatively simple. Using an instrument such as an astrolabe, you measured the angle of a prominent star (or the sun or moon) above the horizon. By comparing this angle with the star's altitude at another, known point (say, your home port), you could calculate how far you were from that point. The problem with this method was that it could only be used in clear weather.

Determining longitude presented a much greater problem. First, early mathematicians severely underestimated the circumference of the Earth, and therefore the distance that each degree of longitude covered. Second, even with careful astronomical observations, longitude could only be worked out precisely if you knew the difference in time between the two points. Unfortunately, the earliest clocks,

which relied on the pendulum, were useless at sea.

By the time Cook set out on his first voyage, the sextant (invented in 1730) allowed mariners to determine latitude with unprecedented accuracy, and make their measurements with one hand while holding the instrument in the other—a great advantage on a moving deck. Scientists had measured a degree of latitude precisely and, with the aid of the telescope, were mapping the heavens and producing much more accurate astronomical tables. Cook also benefited from increasingly comprehensive tables of winds and tides.

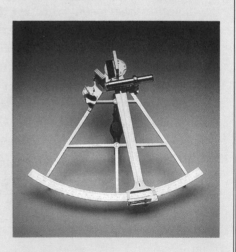

Cook's Sextant

At about the same time, two important advances were made in the calculation of longitude. In 1767, the Astronomer Royal Nevil Maskelyne published his *Natural Almanac*, which set out the times of lunar phases in relation to fixed stars. Navigators could now work out their longitude east or west of Greenwich by comparing the times of these phases given by Maskelyne with the times they observed at sea. This was the method Cook used (and taught to his midshipmen) on the *Endeavour* voyage.

Chronometer K
[Kendall] 3

Harrison in England, and it tested successfully on a voyage to the West Indies in 1761–62. Approving of the device, the Board of Longitude had Larcum Kendall make a copy, which Cook carried on his second voyage. He wrote in his journal for 29 July 1775:

We made the Land about Plymouth; Maker Church, at 5 o'clock in the after-noon, bore N.10° west distant 7 Leagues, this bearing and distance shew that the error of Mr. Kendals Watch in Longitude was only 7'45", which was too far to the west.

A tiny error after the voyage of just over three years.

The age of scientific navigation was at hand.

Astronomical Quadrant

While it did produce accurate results, the calculations involved were complicated and time-consuming, and bad weather could impede observations. The other advance was the development of an instrument that could keep time for long periods at sea. The first accurate marine chronometer was made in 1761 by John lands were uninhabited, he was to 'take possession of them for His Majesty, by setting up proper Marks and Inscriptions as first Discoverers & Possessors'. He was then to survey Pepys's Island and the Falkland Islands for suitable harbours. After wintering either there or at Port Desire on the coast of Patagonia, where he would be resupplied by a storeship, he was to proceed into the Pacific Ocean and sail north to New Albion. There, he was 'to search the said Coast with great care and diligence'. If he found no signs of a passage to Hudson's Bay and the Atlantic, he was to proceed across the Pacific and return to England through the East Indies and via the Cape of Good Hope.

Byron took the *Dolphin* and *Tamar* out from Plymouth on 3 July 1764. At the end of November, he reached Port Desire. After refreshing his ships, he searched the south Atlantic for Pepys Island (which was in fact one of the Falklands misplaced), then retreated to Port Famine in the Strait of Magellan, where he again refreshed. In January 1765 he surveyed and claimed the Falklands, deciding that Port Egmont on the western island was the best site for a base, and unaware that the French explorer Louis Antoine de Bougainville had already formed a settlement on the eastern island. He then met the expected storeship at Port Desire, taking supplies from it and putting on it his report and charts.

Byron then decided not to explore the southern Atlantic towards the Cape of Good Hope for the supposed *Terra Australis*, and also to abandon the probe up the American coast in search of the Northwest Passage. He explained these breaches of his instructions by claiming that the ships were 'too much disabled for the California voyage', and that his intention was therefore 'to run over for India by a new Track'. He wrote in his journal for 9 May 1765: 'I intend if possible to make a NW Course til we get the true Trade wind, and then to shape a Course to the Wtward in hopes of falling in with Solomons Islands if there are such, or else to make some new Discovery.' Until recently, this change in plan seemed inexplicable, but we can now see that what Byron did was to revert to Anson's 1749 scheme, for he sailed north past Juan Fernández until he reached the Tropic of Capricorn, then turned northwest to cross through 100° of longitude (about 10 000 km), before turning north again and crossing the equator at 176° E longitude. Several times in this passage, the absence of the great swell that rolls up the Pacific persuaded him that there was land to the south, but he found none of note as he crossed north of the central atolls. In July, after he turned north, he passed through the Gilbert group, to reach Tinian in the Ladrones at the very end of the month. By stages, he then passed west of the Philippines down to Batavia, and round the Cape of Good Hope. Byron reached England again in May 1766, having made no significant discoveries, but having completed the quickest circumnavigation to date.

The key to the Pacific

Almost a year before, Lord Egmont had received the report and charts which Byron had sent home by the storeship *Florida*. He had then prepared a report for cabinet. Cautioning that the business was one of 'very great Moment & of the most secret nature', he had told his colleagues that the Falkland Islands were

> undoubtedly 'the Key to the whole Pacifick Ocean'. This island must command the Ports & Trade of Chili Peru, Panama, Acapulco, & in one word all the Spanish Territory upon that Sea. It will render all our Expeditions to those parts most lucrative to ourselves, most fatal to Spain, & no longer formidable tedious, or uncertain in a future War.

He went on:

> What farther advantages may be derived from Discoverys in all that Southern Tract of Ocean both to the East & West of the magellanick Streights, it is not possible at present to foresee,

*but those Parts (now almost entirely unknown) will from such
a Settlement be soon & easily explor'd—and a Trade may be
probably carried on with Paraguay, the Brazils &c hereafter
with great Facility, & great Profit from this Island as well in
time of Peace as War.*

Then, offering excerpts from navigators' journals that demonstrated the priority of Britain's claim to the Falklands, Egmont said of the Spanish claim:

*It is impossible that even their pretended Title from the Pope's
grant, or any Treaty . . . can given them the least Claim to an
Island lying 80 or 100 Leagues in the Atlantick Ocean
Eastwards of the Continent of South America, to which it
cannot be deem'd appurtenant.*

Of France's claim (the British now knew about Bougainville's settlement), he said:

*The 1st & 2nd Discoverys of this Island were both made by
the Subjects, & under the authority of the Crown of G. Britain
in the reigns of Q. Elizabeth & Charles the Second, & the
French never saw them till in the reign of Q. Anne. Their
present Projector Frezier owns that they were first discover'd
by the English.*

Cabinet therefore decided to establish a base at Port Egmont on West Falkland; and in October 1765 Captain John McBride and a company of marines sailed to do this. In line with his views on the strategic and commercial importance of the Falklands, Egmont set about familiarising himself with the extensive papers of Henry

Hutchinson, which included details of sailing routes to, and harbours on the coasts of Spain's American colonies, the size and fortifications of their towns, their trade, the political leanings of their inhabitants, and proposals to establish a colony and a free port on the mainland or on an adjacent island. Such a colony might be used to trade British goods for silver and gold, and also to support trade in other regions of the world: 'We might hereafter if Necessary, from this Colony, carry on a Trade to China & the East Indies, without Carrying any Bullion out of Great Britain.'

When Byron returned in May 1766, cabinet quickly decided on a second expedition. On 3 June, Egmont asked his fellow Lords Commissioners of the Admiralty what their views were 'concerning the consideration of the Expedition to Falkland Islands and for Discoveries in the Southern Parts of the World'. They replied 'that if His Majesty thinks fit, the said Discoveries be maintained, and further pursu'd with the addition of one or two Sloops'. This decision was soon given extra importance when on 26 June Egmont received an intelligence report that France hoped to use its Falklands base as a springboard for the discovery of *Terra Australis*. Preparations for a new voyage of circumnavigation were quickly made, and Samuel Wallis sailed out with the *Dolphin* and *Swallow* on 21 August 1766. In a later note, Egmont summarised the motives for this expedition:

Upon Representation of the said Earl to the King, that the Knowledge of the Ports in Falklands Islands, & of the Streights of Magellan would greatly facilitate farther discoveries in the Pacifick Ocean, South of the Line, if pursued, before a War with France or Spain, or the Jealousy of those two Powers should oblige Great Britain to part with the Possession of Falklands Islands, or otherwise Interrupt the attempts of Great Britain in that Part of the world, His Majesty was graciously pleased to Authorize this second Expedition to be undertaken, in hopes of finding a Continent of Great Extent never yet Explored or seen between the Streights of Magellan and New Zeeland.

By the time this second expedition sailed, Britain—as Egmont feared—was again arguing with Spain over the right to navigate and trade in the southern oceans. When he learned of Bougainville's settlement of the Falklands, the Spanish Foreign Minister protested to the French government, and the French Minister of Marine reluctantly agreed to hand over the outpost (which Bougainville did on 1 April 1767). Spain also protested to Britain over its activities in the south Atlantic. In June, upon Byron's return, Prince Masserano, the Spanish Ambassador, took up the business with Egmont and the Duke of Richmond, Secretary of State at the Southern Department, arguing that 'all those countries' the explorer had evidently visited 'are the [Spanish] King's and no one may settle them'. The Duke of Richmond asked in reply 'if the whole world was Spain's', and Masserano answered: 'as to that portion, yes'.

The news that the British were planning a follow-up voyage soon spurred Masserano to sharper protest, for from the first the Spanish believed that their rivals' real purpose was to get into a better position to conduct war and trade with Spain's American colonies. The ambassador was most suspicious when he learned Byron had revisited the island off the coast of Chile where he had been shipwrecked in 1741. He wrote to Madrid: 'As . . . it is very near the mainland, it is to be feared that this would seriously prejudice our commerce should the English establish themselves there, since they would engage in smuggling in the silver which they need for their trade with China.' Late in July, Masserano reported that Byron had suggested the British establish a base on Nukunau in the Gilbert Islands, but that the ministers had chosen instead to 'fix upon the Falkland Islands now that a safe track for the passage through Mageland's Strait has been assured'. The British would use a settlement in the Falklands, he said, to support a covert trade with Brazil, Argentina and perhaps Paraguay, which could be reached by river. They would maintain one armed trading ship on the Atlantic coast and another at the same latitude in the South Sea, 'so as to be within range for making a profit on all sides'. The Falklands settlement would also offer British squadrons a valuable base in time of war against the Spaniards in the region.

The British administration changed in July 1766. Sir Charles

Saunders became First Lord of the Admiralty, and the Earl of Shelburne the Southern Secretary of State. In September, Masserano discussed the business at length with Shelburne. To back up Spain's objection to a British presence in the south Atlantic, he cited the Treaty of Utrecht, in which the European nations had agreed, among other things, to respect the status quo in the Americas established by the papal bulls and the 'Laws of the Indies'. Shelburne said he understood that this agreement excluded merchant vessels from Spain's colonial waters, but not warships. Masserano replied that the presence of warships naturally made Spain suspect British intentions. After the two men each tried to prove to the other that his nation had discovered the Falklands first, they reached the real issues. Producing a map, Shelburne asked Masserano to point out how far Spanish claims extended. Masserano indicated the south Atlantic as far east as the Falklands, 'the islands around Cape Horn towards the coasts of Chile and Peru, as far as Juan Fernández', and the South Seas 'as far as the Philippine Islands'. Shelburne told Masserano that 'Spain's ideas were vast'; Masserano replied that Britain's were 'still greater'.

Shelburne then set out his final position:

That the right of Navigation was so indisputably of our side, that I could not consent to talk seriously upon it. That if the Spaniards talking of their Possessions included the A[merican] and S[outh] Seas, and that our navigating them gave occasion to them to Suspect a War, I had no hesitation to say that I would advise one if they insisted on reviving such a vague & strange pretension, long since wore out, as the exclusive right of those Seas.

With that, he defined what was to remain one of the fundamental determinants of Pacific exploration until the end of the eighteenth century.

Britain and Spain continued their argument over the settlement of the Falkland Islands for some years. In June 1770, in a move that would be eerily echoed just over 200 years later, a Spanish force from Buenos Aires captured Port Egmont. Britain then mobilised its navy for war, but Lord North, the prime minister, secretly offered to abandon the outpost if Spain first gave it back to Britain. Spain accepted, and both these things were done in 1774.

2

EDEN IN THE PACIFIC

The discovery of Tahiti, and French voyages,

1766–1773

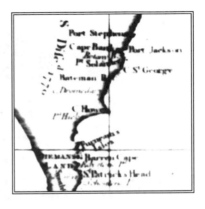

The British were able to accept the loss of their very modest base on West Falkland because continued exploration had turned up a potentially much more useful site. The 1766 expedition commanded by Captain Samuel Wallis was instructed to focus on the southern Pacific rather than the southern Atlantic, and search for 'that Land, or Islands of great extent, hitherto unvisited by any European Power . . . between Cape Horn and New Zeland'. Wallis was

to proceed with the Dolphin and Swallow round Cape Horn or through the Streights of Magellan . . . and Stretch to the Westward about One Hundred or One Hundred and Twenty Degrees of Longitude from Cape Horn, loosing as little Southing as Possible, in Search of the Land or Islands supposed to lie in that part of the Southern Hemisphere which is before mentioned, unless you shall discover such Land or Islands in a Shorter Run.

Like Byron before him, if he found land Wallis was to study it carefully; make friends with the indigenous inhabitants if possible; purchase suitable sites for bases from them; or 'if no Inhabitants are found on the land or Islands so discovered, you are . . . to take Possession of such Land or Islands so discovered for His Majesty, by setting up proper Marks and Inscriptions as first Discoverers and Possessors'.

The Dolphin's *arrival at Matavia Bay, 1767.*
So far as we know, the Dolphin's *visit to Tahiti was the first by Europeans.*
The culture shock was mutual as both the Native Tahitians and the Stranger
Europeans sought to incorporate the other into their cosmic and social systems.

With Lieutenant Philip Carteret commanding the *Swallow*, Wallis sailed from Plymouth in the *Dolphin* on 22 August 1776. The two ships entered the Straits of Magellan in mid-December, but became separated during the passage and did not meet up again on the voyage. Wallis crossed the Pacific a few degrees to the south of Byron's route, and discovered Tahiti. So far as we know, he and his crew were the first Europeans to experience this delightful island. Their introduction to its pleasures, however, was decidedly odd.

As the *Dolphin* coasted the island, the Natives came out in their canoes, first to proffer fronds of plantain and long speeches, which the Strangers took as gestures of good will, then to trade food for the Strangers' goods, particularly nails and other metal items. Repeatedly, the Natives tried to persuade the Strangers to bring the ship inshore and to land, including by having 'Young Girls play a great many droll want[on] tricks'. When the Strangers would not oblige, the Natives pelted them with stones.

This scene was re-enacted on a much larger scale when Wallis at last decided to enter Matavai Bay—as George Robertson, the ship's master, described it:

> *At sun rise about three hundred canoes came off and lay round the ship, as many as could conveniently lay allongside traded very fair and took nails and Toys for their Hogs, fowls and fruit, by Eight oclock their was upwards of five hundred canoes round the ship, and at a Moderate Computation there was near four thousand men—the most of the trading canoes which lay round the ship, and dealt with our people, had a fair young Girl in Each Canoe, who playd a great many droll wanton tricks, which drew all our people upon the Gunwells to see them, when they seemd to be most merry and friendly some of our people observd great numbers of stones in every canoe, this created a little suspition in several of our people, but the most of us could not think they hade any Bade Intention against us, Espetially as the whole traded very fair and honest, and all the men seemd as hearty and merry as the Girls.*

Then a signal was raised from a large canoe in which sat 'several of the Principle Inhabitance'. Instantly,

> *all trade broke up, and in a few secants of time all our Decks was full of Great and small stones, and several of our men cut and Bruisd this was so sudden and unexpected by the most of us, that we was some time before we could find out the caus, therefor orderd the sentrys to fire amongst them, in hopes that would frighten them, but this hade not the desired Effect, they all gave another shout and powerd in the stones lyke hail amongst us which hurt a great many of our men, we then*

19

found lenity would not do, therefor applyed to the Great Guns and gave them a few round and Grape shot, which struck such terror amongs the poor unhapy croad that it would require the pen of Milton to describe, therefore too mutch for mine. When any of the round shot took their canoes it caried all before it, and the poor unhappy creatures that escaped immediately Jumpt overboard and hung by the remaining part of the canoe, untill some of their friends took them up or towed off the Brockin canoe, when we found they all puld off, we gave over firing for some time, and enquired how this affear began.

There was another serious conflict three days later, when Wallis ordered cannon balls fired into the people crowded on a hill over-looking the bay, then had the crew split the bottoms of eighty canoes so as to prevent a night attack on the ship. The next day, the Natives again offered plantains and food, and after that relations settled down, trade was established, and the Strangers were able to land their many scurvy-afflicted sick and restore them with fresh food.

Today we know that the Polynesians viewed the *Dolphin* as the great canoe of the god 'Oro, who legend said had first come from the land beyond the sky and would one day return. Coincidentally, the major temple of 'Oro in Tahiti was at Matavai Bay, so that when the ship anchored there, the Natives believed the god had come to visit them. The plantain fronds they held out to the Strangers were symbolic of human sacrifice, and therefore offerings to 'Oro, and the 'Principal Inhabitant' who directed the attack was the chief priest of 'Oro's temple; his large canoe was 'Rainbow', the arc in which 'Oro's symbols were carried. The Natives' desperate attempts—food, girls—to entice the Strangers on shore were intended to obtain the benefit of 'Oro's *mana* (status, power) and the gifts he had brought. Their stone-throwing was a sign of their resentment at the Strangers' refusal to oblige.

Once peaceful relations were established, the Europeans were able to move freely about the island, which to them seemed a paradise. For one thing, the entire island seemed, as master's mate John Gore wrote, to be a bountiful garden:

for the first two miles [the river] flowed through a valley of considerable width, in which were many habitations, with gardens walled in, and abundance of hogs, poultry, and fruit; the soil here seemed to be a rich fat earth, and was of a blackish colour. After this the valley became very narrow, and the ground rising abruptly on one side of the river, we were all obliged to march on the other. Where the stream was precipitated from the hills, channels had been cut to lead the water into gardens and plantations of fruit trees . . . The ground was fenced off so as to make a very pretty appearance; the bread-fruit and apple trees were planted in rows on the declivity of the hills, and the cocoa nut and plantain, which require more moisture, on the level ground.

The European men also found the Tahitian women astonishingly willing to have sex. The price of this favour was quickly established as a nail, and so frenetic did the trade become that Wallis had to forbid the crew from drawing nails from the ship, for fear it might fall apart. In the end, he refused to let the men go ashore except in working parties. It is easy for us with our modern consciousness to see this trade as evidence of how Europeans inevitably corrupt non-Europeans, and as a sign of how Polynesian culture was blighted from that time on. But we should also be aware that, given their potential for use as fishhooks, knives and spears, nails were a particularly valuable commodity in a metal-less culture, and that as soon as they realised this, the Tahitians used the most effective means they knew of to obtain them. That is, the Tahitians were as eager to participate in the trade as were the Europeans.

After five weeks, Wallis headed westward again for 2000 km before turning north for the Ladrones. Going southward through the East Indies and rounding the Cape of Good Hope, he reached

⊰ LIFE AT SEA: BOOZE AND BOREDOM ⊱

Anyone who has not toured the new *Endeavour* might find it hard to imagine what it was like to sail on an eighteenth-century ship of exploration. Well built and well equipped as many of these vessels were, they were still comparatively small. The *Endeavour*, for example, was 106 feet (32.3 m) long overall—67 feet 7 inches (29.7 m) on the lower deck—and 29 feet 3 inches (8.9 m) wide.

Cut out of the Endeavour

Into ships like this were crammed food and equipment for up to three years, and about 100 officers, seamen and 'supernumeraries' (i.e., scientists, artists, servants). While the commander might be comfortably, and the officers reasonably, accommodated, the men's quarters were usually extremely crowded, with little or no headroom in the hold, and hammocks strung close together.

The need to carry unusual items such as plants and animals made this problem even more acute. The 1000 breadfruit plants on the *Bounty* took up already very limited space, and Bligh fussed obsessively over them, thus causing further resentment in an already unhappy crew. And Johann Forster left a harrowing description of how, on the *Resolution*, Cook housed animals near the cabins in an effort to spare them from seasickness:

I was now beset with cattle & stench on both sides, having no other but a thin deal partition full of chinks between me and them. The room offered me by Capt. Cook, & which the Masters obstinacy deprived me of, was now given to very peacably bleating creatures, who on a stage raised up as high as my bed, shit & pissed on one side, whichst five Goats did the same afore on the other side.

In these circumstances, tempers flared, and alcohol only exacerbated the problem. While the *Endeavour* was moving up the east Australian coast, Cook wrote:

Last Night some time in the Middle watch a very extraordinary affair happend to Mr [Richard] Orton my Clerk, he having been drinking in the Evening, some Malicious person or persons in the Ship took the advantage of his being drunk and cut off all the cloaths from off his back, not being satisfied with this they some time after went into his Cabbin and cut off a part of both his Ears as he lay asleep in his bed.

Officers were just as susceptible to alcohol's influence as the men were. William Bayly, the astronomer on the *Resolution*, recorded how one evening in March 1773:

After I was in bed, Mr Kempe the 1st Lieutenant, & Mr Burney 2nd Lieutenant, Mr Andrews the Surgeon, & Mr Hawksey Midshipman all came to my door and asked me to give them brandy which I refused to do, thinking they already had had enough, it being between 12 o'clock and 1 o'clock at night, and begged them to go to bed. But they procured a hammer and chisel and began ripping the hinges off my door.

When Bayly opened his door, his visitors assaulted him.

Aside from alcohol, seamen looked for comfort to their pets, such as birds, cats and monkeys, but these too often caused trouble. On the second voyage, Cook threw a number of monkeys overboard when they fouled the ship, and Banks permitted no animals at all on Bligh's breadfruit voyages (which he organised), for fear of the damage they might do to the plants.

Boredom was a constant feature of shipboard life. Seamen whiled away their time carving wood or bone or gambling. Officers talked and drank together, played backgammon and wrote up their journals. Commanders sometimes organised entertainment, inviting the officers to dine with them, and making the crew exercise regularly, including by dancing on the deck.

The full extent of homosexuality at sea is unknown, but if modern segregated prisons are any indication, it was probably common. Once in port, wise commanders such as Bougainville and Cook knew it would be foolish to forbid the sailors from having sexual encounters with women. An inventive 'gentleman' might not even have to wait until he reached port. Before he decided to pull out of Cook's second voyage (after an argument over how much space he and his entourage would occupy on the overloaded *Resolution*), Joseph Banks sent a woman who dressed as a man ahead to Madeira, where she was to join the ship as his 'servant'.

England again in May 1768. In March the following year, Carteret too finally returned. Having crossed into the western Pacific south of Wallis's route, he had missed Tahiti but re-found the Solomon Islands (discovered by Alvaro de Mendaña in 1568, but not precisely located because of error in the calculation of longitude).

From the time Carteret had reached the western Pacific, disaster threatened to overwhelm his ship. Scurvy made great inroads among the crew, who were by this time very short of provisions. At Santa Cruz, Melanesians attacked a landing party which violated *tapu* (taboo) by cutting down a coconut tree, killing four and wounding others. The loss of an officer and of several of the healthier men meant that if Carteret, who was himself very ill, had died, there would have been only one officer capable of directing the ship home, and few seamen capable of working it. Dispirited, Carteret decided to abandon further exploration and headed above New Guinea for the East Indies. As he went, scurvy continued to strike the crew down; there were repeated clashes with the inhabitants of the islands at which they desperately tried to obtain food and water; and the *Swallow* became more and more decrepit as they encountered heavy storms: 'this was extreemly fatigueing to our poor reduced sickly Crew, for with all hands that were able to remain without distinction on this pressing necessary Occasion, it was the utmost we could do to muster strength enough to hand the sails, we were now scarce a day without some falling sick or dying'. After refreshing in the East Indies and at the Cape of Good Hope, Carteret made his slow way up the Atlantic. Near Ascension Island in the mid-Atlantic, he encountered Bougainville, who observed: 'His ship was very small, went very ill, and when we took leave of him, he remained as it were at anchor. How much he must have suffered in so bad a vessel, may well be conceived.'

Bougainville himself was also drawing near the end of a circumnavigation. When France had decided to meet Spain's wishes concerning the Falklands, the Minister of Marine had given him two naval vessels, the frigate *Boudeuse* and the storeship *Etoile*, and instructed him to hand over the settlement he had founded and evacuate the colonists before going on to explore in the Pacific Ocean. Reflecting the intellectual climate of the Enlightenment,

Bougainville took scientists with him—the naturalist Philibert de Commerson and the astronomer Pierre-Antoine Véron.

He sailed from France in November 1766 and relinquished his Falklands settlement to the Spanish on 1 April 1767. After refreshing at Rio de Janeiro, he sailed again in November, and passed through the Straits of Magellan into the Pacific on 26 January 1768. Like all the navigators before him, he found it impossible to head directly west in the face of opposing winds and currents, so he took the now usual path, heading north until near the Tropic of Capricorn, and then, with the trade winds behind him, gently northwest. This route brought him through the Tuamotu Archipelago to Tahiti in early April 1768, some nine months after Wallis.

Having learned from the earlier visit what the Strangers liked and what goods they had to offer, the Tahitians swarmed out to the French ships, their canoes laden with food and women. Bougainville wrote of their arrival:

As we came nearer the shore, the number of islanders surrounding our ships encreased. The periaguas [canoes] were so numerous all about the ships, that we had much to do to warp in amidst the croud of boats and the noise. All these people came crying out tayo, which means friend, and gave a thousand signs of friendship; they all asked nails and ear-rings of us. The periaguas were full of females; who, for agreeable features, are not inferior to most European women; and who in point of beauty of the body might, with much reason, vie with them all. Most of these fair females were naked; for the men and the old women that accompanied them, had stripped them of the garments which they generally dress themselves in. The glances which they gave us from their periaguas, seemed to discover some degree of uneasiness, notwithstanding the innocent manner in which they were given; perhaps, because nature has every where embellished their sex with a natural timidity; or because even in those countries, where the ease of the golden age is still in use, women seem least to desire what they most wish for.

The men, who were more plain, or rather more free, soon
explained their meaning very clearly. They pressed us to choose
a woman, and to come on shore with her; and their gestures,
which were nothing less than equivocal, denoted in what
manner we should form an acquaintance with her. It was very
difficult, amidst such a sight, to keep at their work four
hundred young French sailors, who had seen no women for six
months. In spite of all our precautions, a young girl came on
board, and placed herself upon the quarter-deck, near one of the
hatchways, which was open, in order to give air to those who
were heaving at the capstern below it. The girl carelessly dropt
a cloth, which covered her, and appeared to the eyes of all
beholders, such as Venus shewed herself to the Phrygian
shepherd, having, indeed, the celestial form of that goddess.
Both sailors and soldiers endeavoured to come to the
hatch-way; and the capstern was never hove with more alacrity
than on this occasion.

Bougainville stayed at Tahiti only for ten days, but during this
short time the Tahitians so lavished their hospitality upon the
Europeans that he named it Nouvelle Cythère (New Cythera), after
the Greek island said to be the birthplace of Aphrodite, the goddess
of love (whom the Romans knew as Venus). In his account of his
voyage, he portrayed the island as an earthly paradise and as the
home of the 'Good Savage', one of whom—Aotourou (Ahutoru)—
he took back to France for evidence.

From Tahiti, Bougainville sailed almost due west, finding the
Samoan Islands, re-finding the New Hebrides (discovered by Pedro
Fernández de Quirós in 1606 and named by him Austrialia del
Espiritu Santo). Continuing west in hopes of discovering at last the
fabled southern continent, or at least the east coast of New Holland,
he reached the Great Barrier Reef, against which 'the sea broke with
great violence'. Bougainville saw the breakers as 'the voice of God'
warning him of danger. It was a warning he chose to obey, retreating
eastwards until he was able to sail north of New Guinea to the East

Indies. With his crew now preferring the ship's rats to their rotten provisions, he went through the Louisiade Archipelago and the Solomon Islands to Batavia and then the Cape of Good Hope. As he proceeded up the Atlantic towards Europe, he came across Carteret, whom he offered to help as he could. But with national interest firmly in mind, neither commander gave the other details of where he had been in the Pacific.

From the point of view of European ships plying the vast Pacific Ocean, Tahiti, with its central location and lavish food resources, was a great find. And rumour soon gave the island extra fascination. When the *Dolphin* reached the Cape of Good Hope, some of the crew could not help talking about where they had been, and it was soon being said that 'an English vessel had found in the South Sea a very rich island where, among other peculiarities, a colony of Jews had been settled'. (This last idea seems to have arisen from the fact that the Tahitians practised circumcision.)

Thinking that this island might be identical with the one that Henry Davis had reportedly seen in 1686 at 28°S latitude and 100°W longitude, the French navigator Jean de Surville and his merchant backers decided to establish trade with it and, indeed, to colonise it. Surville left from Pondicherry in India on 2 June 1769, on a voyage which ended disastrously. He first took the *St Jean-Baptiste* through the Straits of Malacca up to the Bashi Islands off the south coast of China. Then, rounding the northern Philippines, he sailed southeast to the Solomon Islands, where one of his crew was killed and others wounded in a conflict with Melanesians. Surville continued south past New Caledonia to the vicinity of Lord Howe Island, then went east, reaching Doubtless Bay on the northern tip of New Zealand on 17 December, with many of the crew dead or desperately ill with scurvy. (At one point he and James Cook, then circumnavigating New Zealand, were probably only about 50 km apart, but did not see each other.) Deciding to give up the idea of settling a colony on Tahiti, and to head for the west coast of South America instead, Surville sailed again on 31 December. Taking an erratic route between 34° and 40°S latitude, he went where none but Cook had been before, but found no sign of the southern continent. Scurvy renewed its ravages, and by the

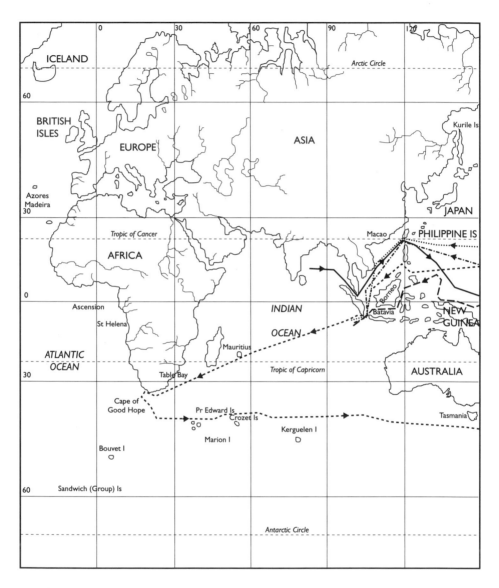

Eighteenth Century Voyages of Pacific Exploration, I: Byron 1764–6, Wallis 1766–8,

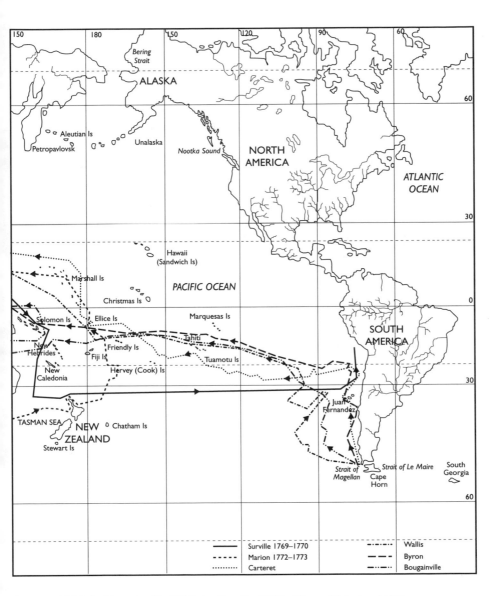

Carteret 1766–9, Bougainville 1766–9, Surville 1769–70, and Marion 1772.

time he sighted the American coast on 4 April, many more of his crew were either dead or on the point of death. Desperate to obtain help, Surville tried to cross the bar of Chilca harbour in one of the ship's boats, but drowned in the heavy seas. Guillaume Labé, the first officer, took the *St Jean-Baptiste* into Callao harbour on 9 April, where Spanish authorities detained it and its remaining crew for three years.

There was another French expedition to the Pacific in the early 1770s. In 1771, Marc-Joseph Marion Dufresne, preparing to carry Autourou back to Tahiti, decided to take the opportunity to pursue an ambitious scheme to discover *Terra Australis*: 'I shall set my course . . . to reconnoitre the southern lands and find out if they exist, as I think they do.' Marion sailed from Mauritius in two ships, the *Mascarin* and the *Marquis de Castries*, on 18 October 1771. He went first to Madagascar, where Autourou died of smallpox. The expedition reached the Cape of Good Hope at the beginning of December, then looked fruitlessly for a landmass in the southern Indian Ocean. On 6 March 1772, the ships anchored in North Bay, Tasmania, where the crews became the first Europeans to see that island's inhabitants.

Marion then decided to cross to New Zealand. He sighted the west coast of the north island at Mt Egmont on 25 March, then, skirting north, reached the Bay of Islands at the beginning of May. There, after some initial friendly contact and trade, in mid-June Maori killed Marion and two boats' crews. In retaliation, the French killed more than 200 Maori. The subordinate officers took the ships to sea again on 12 July and headed north to Guam and Manila before returning through the East Indies to Mauritius in April 1773.

3

AN EXPLORER'S DESTINY

James Cook's first voyage, 1768–1771

As important as the find of Tahiti was, Samuel Wallis returned to England believing that he had made an infinitely greater one. In the days before they reached Tahiti and just after they left it, he and his crew thought they saw the cloud-hung fringe of the fabled southern continent, but because they had only one ship, Wallis decided 'it was too hazardous . . . to coast the Continent (which they had then actually in View). And afterwards [they] thought [it] most prudent on their Return, not to take Notice that they had Ever seen it at all'. So when Wallis returned to England, indications were that another voyage would result in a momentous geographical discovery.

As it happened, another voyage was already in preparation. The planet Venus was to cross the sun on 3 June 1769. European scientists were extremely keen to observe this phenomenon, for if they could obtain a precise measurement of the time the transit took, they would be able to calculate accurately the distance of the Earth from the sun. This knowledge would also be helpful for navigation. The more broadly spread the points of observation were, the more accurate the measurements would be. And the transit would be easier to observe in the southern than in the northern hemisphere. The British Royal Society therefore planned to send two astronomers to Lapland's North Cape, two to Hudson's Bay, and two to an island in the Pacific. In 1768, the Society persuaded King George III to provide £4000 and a Royal Navy ship to carry the latter two out. Plans for the voyage were well advanced when Wallis returned in May 1768. The ship had been chosen and was being fitted out, and officers and scientific observers were being appointed. The ship was a Whitby collier, a 'cat-built' bark of 368 tons called the *Earl of Pembroke*, chosen not for its sailing speed (which was slow) but for its broad, shallow build, which enabled it to carry the large quantity of stores needed for a long voyage, and at the same time to sail reasonably close inshore. For this expedition, it was renamed *Endeavour*. Its commander and one of the astronomers was Lieutenant James Cook; Charles Green was the other astronomer; and at the request of the Royal Society, the young botanist Joseph Banks was also to sail. At his own expense, Banks would take a scientific entourage, including the botanist Dr Daniel Solander, to help him collect specimens, and the artists Sydney Parkinson, Alexander Buchan and Herman Spöring to produce botanical, zoological and ethnographic drawings.

When Wallis announced his discovery of Tahiti, it sounded like an ideal site for observing the transit, and the Royal Society and the Admiralty quickly made the island the expedition's first major destination. Because of the *Endeavour* voyage's origins, because of the skill Cook displayed in navigation and charting during it, and because of the wonderful collections Banks and Solander returned with, twentieth-century historians have tended to stress the expedition's scientific character. Certainly, from this point of view it was a striking achievement. But I believe the Admiralty found it convenient to add to the voyage's purpose because, with Lord Sandwich again at their head, the Lords Commissioners saw what a great opportunity it offered to complete the discovery of *Terra Australis* and continue Anson's and Egmont's scheme to establish a series of bases and a commercial empire in and around the Pacific Ocean.

Wallis's report of having seen a continental coastline to the south of Tahiti was central to the secret instructions the Admiralty gave to Cook:

Whereas there is reason to imagine that a Continent or Land of great extent, may be found to the Southward of the Tract lately made by Captn. Wallis in His Majesty's Ship the

*Dolphin (of which you will herewith receive a Copy) or of the
Tract of any former Navigators in Pursuits of the like kind;
You are therefore in Pursuance of His Majesty's Pleasure hereby
requir'd and directed to put to Sea with the Bark you
Command so soon as the Observation of the Transit of the
Planet Venus shall be finished and observe the
following Instructions.*

If he found this continent, Cook was to chart it carefully and record
the nature of its soil, animals and plants. He was

*to observe the Genius, Temper, Disposition and Number of
the Natives, if there be any, and endeavour by all proper
means to cultivate a Friendship and Alliance with them,
making them presents of such Trifles as they may Value,
inviting them to Traffick, and Shewing them every kind of
Civility and Regard.*

And he was 'with the Consent of the Natives to take possession of
Convenient Situations in the Country in the Name of the King of
Great Britain; or, if you find the Country uninhabited take Posses-
sion for His Majesty by setting up Proper Marks and Inscriptions,
as first discoverers and possessors'. If he failed to locate *Terra
Australis*, he was to chart New Zealand and then return via either
Cape Horn or the Cape of Good Hope.

Where none had been before

Whatever balance we strike between imperial ambitions and scientific ideals in the British exploration of the Pacific, there can be no
disagreement about the importance of James Cook. Cook was one

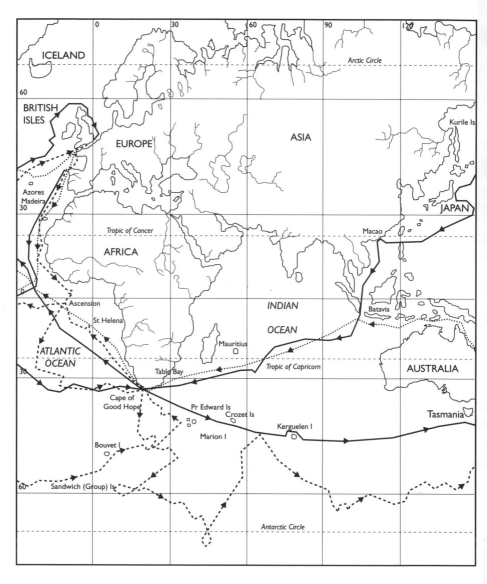

Eighteenth Century Voyages of Pacific Exploration, II: Three Voyages of Captain

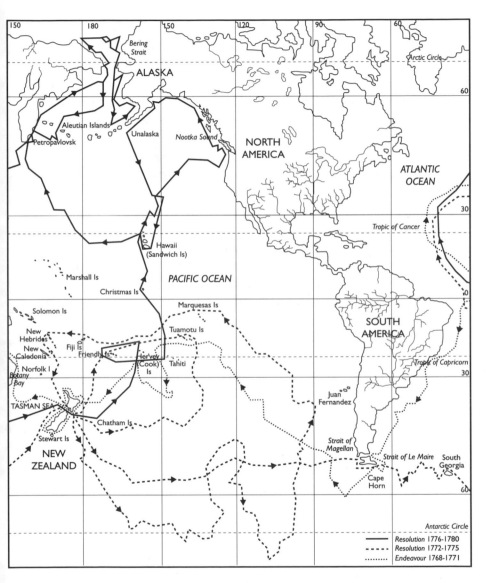

Cook, 1768–71, 1772–5 and 1776–80.

of the most extraordinary people of his age, yet he came from a lowly background and had no formal education. He was born on 27 October 1728 in the village of Marsden, Yorkshire, where his father was a day-labourer. As an apprentice in the North Sea coal trade, Cook began to learn the principles of navigation, mathematics and astronomical observation. When the Seven Years War broke out in 1755, he joined the Royal Navy, serving mostly in North America, where he continued his self-education and distinguished himself by his diligent and accurate charting of the St Lawrence River and the coasts of Nova Scotia and Newfoundland, and by the observation of an eclipse of the sun. Together with the powerful patronage of Sir Hugh Palliser, these qualifications persuaded the Admiralty to offer Cook the command of the *Endeavour*.

The *Endeavour* sailed from Plymouth on 26 August 1768, making Madeira on 12 September, Rio de Janeiro on 14 November, and entering the Pacific at the end of January 1769. In his passage from Cape Horn to Tahiti Cook took 'a far more westerly Track than any Ship had ever done before', but he found no land until he neared the island. On 13 April he anchored in Matavai Bay. Apart from the annoyance and inconvenience of the Tahitians' kleptomania, relations between the Natives and the Strangers were excellent. Food was plentiful and cheaply bought, the Tahitian women were as generous to the *Endeavour*'s men as they had been to the *Dolphin*'s, and the weather was clear for the astronomical observations, which modern re-evaluation shows were more accurate than has long been thought.

Cook left Tahiti on 13 July. For a month he cruised among the Society Islands. Then, following instructions, on 15 August he headed directly south 'in search of the Continent'. He held this course until 2 September when, in the face of heavy gales and seeing no signs of land, he turned northeast, and after three days, northwest. He turned southwest on 21 September, and sighted the east coast of New Zealand on 7 October. By March 1770 he had circumnavigated and charted its two large islands. Now ready to sail for home, he decided, given the season and the condition of the ship, to return via the East Indies, which he would reach by running west to the east coast of New Holland and following it north. With

The Endeavour *being careened*
The Endeavour's *near wreck on one of the platform reefs inside the Great*
Barrier Reef showed the danger of mounting a distant exploring expedition with
one ship only. Cook spent six weeks repairing the ship, before proceeding on to
Batavia. During this sojourn, the Europeans had their first sight of kangaroos.

this decision, he began to move from competence to greatness, for this route would take him where none had been before.

Cook left New Zealand on 1 April 1770, sighted the east coast of Australia on 19 April, and turned north. In June he nearly lost the *Endeavour* on a reef. After beaching it for repairs, he continued slowly north, first outside the Great Barrier Reef, and then inside it once more. On 16 August, the *Endeavour* narrowly escaped being wrecked a second time. Five days later, at Possession Island, Cook took possession of the east coast of 'New South Wales' in the name of King George III. Then he swung northwest into Torres Strait. After coasting southern New Guinea, he reached Batavia on 2 October, and from there made his way to England, to anchor in the Downs, off east Kent, on 13 July 1771.

Such a brief recital hardly does justice to a voyage that was remarkable for a number of reasons. The geographical accomplishments—the identification of the two main islands of New Zealand, the tracing of the eastern coast of Australia, and the re-finding of Torres Strait—were certainly impressive. As Cook himself said, 'I . . . have made no very great Discoveries[,] yet I have exploar'd more of the Great South Sea than all that have gone before me[,] so much that little remains now to be done to have a thorough knowledge of that part of the Globe'. But there was also Cook's consistent use of the lunar tables worked out by Astronomer Royal Neville Maskelyne, which showed that it was possible to calculate longitude at sea much more accurately than ever before (even if this did involve tedious hours of mathematics). The voyage is also remarkable for Cook's control of scurvy, though recent research has shown that while Cook's insistence on keeping his crew clean, dry and warm, and on feeding them fresh foods whenever in port, effectively kept the disease at bay, he did not understand that citrus juices (with their vitamin C) were what prevented it.

Above all, though, there is the matter of the man himself. The James Cook who sailed the *Endeavour* from England in August 1768 was a man whose view of the world had been shaped by the ideals of the scientific Enlightenment. He had raised himself from the humblest origin to a position of some eminence. He had learnt mathematics, astronomy and navigation until he was more than competent in the subjects. He had surveyed and charted sections of the North American coastline with unprecedented accuracy. He had observed an eclipse of the sun. This James Cook applied his precise and practical habits of mind to everything he did. As a result, he embarked on one of the most momentous voyages in human history without any particular excitement or anticipation. 'At 2 pm got under sail and put to sea having on board 94 persons including Officers Seamen Gentlemen and their servants, near 18 months provisions, 10 Carriage guns 12 Swivels with good store of Ammunition and stores of all kinds,' he wrote in his journal for 26 August 1768, the day he sailed from England. Yet this same James Cook, who described himself as a man without 'the advantage of Education, acquired', and as one who wrote 'for information and not for amusement', was also a man capable of profound imaginative change. In the end, I believe he owed his greatness to this capacity.

The nature of the change which the Pacific Ocean wrought in Cook can be glimpsed in the journal he kept on the first circumnavigation. At the beginning of the voyage Cook used words as he used the other tools of his craft—for precision, as a means to describe, catalogue, and categorise. 'The *Peak of Teneriff*,' he wrote in the entry for 24 September 1768, 'is a very high mountain upon the Island of the same name, one of the Canarie Islands, its perpendicular hight from actual measurement is said to be 15 396 feet. It lies in the Latd. of 28°13'N and Longitude 16°32' West from Greenwich, its situation in this respect is allowed to be pretty well determined.' In writing up his journal, Cook also drew heavily at first on the journal of the better educated and more sophisticated Joseph Banks. But as he changed in the face of the Pacific experience, his intellectual dependence on Banks diminished, and he learned to use words in what was for him a new way, to express imaginative perception and truth. Cook had pretty much stopped borrowing from Banks for his journal by the time they reached New Zealand, where he wrote of the southern Alps:

> *[they] are of a prodigious height and appear to consist of nothing but barren rocks, cover'd in many places with large patches of snow which perhaps have laid their sence the creation. No country upon earth can appear with a more ruged and barren aspect than this doth from the sea for as far inland as the eye can reach nothing is to be seen but the sumits of these Rocky mountains which seem to lay so near one another as not to admit any Vallies between them.*

Whereas Cook's description of the Peak of Tenerife was an exact but unevocative list of measurements, his description of the New Zealand Alps shows him making a sensitive effort to suggest the intangible, as well as the physical, nature of things. Between the first description and the second lay a Pacific crossing.

The change in the quality of Cook's journal reflects the larger imaginative change in Cook, to which the Pacific was central. First, in Tahiti, Cook encountered an 'unnatural' experience which only the officers and men of the *Dolphin* and of Bougainville's expedition had faced before. Cook had no doubt talked with Wallis, he had some of the *Dolphin*'s officers and men in his crew, and he had a copy of Wallis's journal; but he had inherited no real tradition of

❧ DISCIPLINE: HALF RATIONS AND THE LASH ❧

One of the biggest causes of indiscipline on Cook's voyages was food. Men who (as Banks noted with awe when the *Endeavour* struck inside the Great Barrier Reef) were capable of working with great vigour and discipline in a crisis could become mightily unhappy where food was concerned.

On the first voyage, at Madeira, Cook gave two sailors twelve lashes each 'for refusing to take their allowance of fresh Beef'. The men hated sauerkraut, and Cook (believing it was important to prevent scurvy) had to use considerable cunning to get them to eat it:

The Sour Krout the Men at first would note eate untill I put in practice a Method I never once knew to fail with seamen, and this was to have some of it dress'd every Day for the Cabbin Table, and permitted all the Officers without exception to make use of it and left it to the option of the Men either to take as much as they pleased or none atall; but this pratice was not continued above a week before I found it necessary to put every one on board to an Allowance.

Theft was a serious problem on board ship. As Nicholas Rodger has put it: 'Because ships were paid just before sailing, men often had large sums in cash in their possession, with little privacy or security to protect it. A thief among the ship's company destroyed its mutual bonds of trust and loyalty more swiftly than anything else.' Theft was therefore one of the crimes at sea most severely punished. And it was not confined to men's possessions. In June 1769, at Tahiti, Cook punished one seaman with twelve lashes 'for takeing Rum out of the Cast on the quarter deck'. And on the second voyage, the astronomer William Bayly complained bitterly that 'my cask of Porter (which was stowed in the fore

---

Tahiti. For Englishmen, this tradition was to begin with the publication of John Hawkesworth's *An Account of the Voyages undertaken by the order of his present Majesty for making Discoveries in the Southern Hemisphere* (1773). To all practical purposes, Cook discovered Tahiti all over again in 1769. As a result of that experience he changed in a way in which Wallis and Bougainville had not changed; and he changed to a degree impossible even for Banks, who had more intimate contact with the Tahitians than Cook did.

Tahiti engaged Cook's scientific curiosity. He found much that

Hold) was entirely drank out by some of the Ships crew unknown, as likewis a quarter cast of Madeira wine belonging to Mr Shank our late First Lieut.'

When a thief would not own up, Cook sometimes cut everyone's rations to try to smoke him out. As punishment for a theft on the third voyage, as they left New Zealand in March 1777 Cook placed the ships' companies, who had been on two-thirds allowance of biscuit for almost four months, on two-thirds allowance of salt meat as well. James King wrote:

they all refused taking it, thinking it unjust to be punished for no crime of theirs; upon which the Captn told them he look'd upon this refusal as a very mutinous proceeding & that as the honest men would not themselves try to find out the thieves, for there must be many, he should not only put them at

2/3 Allowance the day after, but that it should continue, & that they also should be deprived of having their meat raw.

Cook also cut rations in response to insubordination. In Hawaii in December 1778, the crew of the *Resolution* repeatedly refused to drink the sugar cane beer Cook had had brewed, alleging 'it was injurious to their healths'. On 10 December, after three days of mutinous rumblings, they sent a letter to him, again refusing to drink the beer and complaining about being on short rations while in sight of islands blessed with food. The next day Cook withdrew their grog ration, and on 12 December flogged the cooper for emptying a cask of the beer which had gone sour.

Another common misdemeanor was 'uncleanness'—relieving oneself in the hold rather than at the heads, which was always a temptation in wet, cold and rough conditions.

was fascinating. There was the island itself, which he later described as a 'Terrestrial Paridise'. As he left Tahiti, Cook ended his precise description of it and its produce by noting that

All these articles the Earth almost spontaniously produces or at least they are rais'd with very little labour, in the article of food these people may almost be said to be exempt from the curse of our fore fathers; scarcely can it be said that they earn

their bread with the sweet of their brow, benevolent nature hath not only supply'd them with necessarys but with abundance of superfluities.

There were also the island's inhabitants:

They have all fine white teeth and for the most part short flat noses and thick lips, yet their features are agreable and their gate gracefull, and their behavour to strangers and to each other is open affable and courtious and from all I could see free from treachery.

There were the Tahitians' social customs, such as open burial and the segregation of the sexes at meals, and their sexual mores—the way the young women offered themselves to Banks, the pair who copulated in front of the ship's crew, and the lascivious dancing:

The young girls . . . dance a very indecent dance which they call Timorodee singing most indecent songs and useing most indecent actions in the pratice of which they are brought up from their earlyest Childhood . . . this exercise is however generaly left of as soon as they arrive at years of maturity for as soon as they have form'd a connection with man they are expected to leave of dancing Timorodee.

Cook's curiosity increasingly outweighed any initial repugnance he may have felt. He first wrote of the *Maui* which he and Banks saw during their circumnavigation of the island:

we meet with an Effigy or Figure of a Man made of Basket work & covered with white and Black feathers placed in such order as to represent the Colour of their Hair, & Skins when Tattow'd or painted, it was 7½ feet high & the whole made in due proportion on its head were 4 Nobs not unlike the stumps of large Horns 3 stood in front & one behind we were not able to learn what use they made of this Monster it did not at all appear to us that they paid it the least Homage as a God they were not the least Scrupulous of letting us examine every part of it. I am inclinable to think that it is only used by way of diversion at their Heva's or public entertainments as Punch is in a Puppet show.

But when he described the *Maui* later in his journal, he wrote:

we proceeded farther and met with a very extraordinary curiosity call'd Mahuwe and said by the Natives to be used in their Heiva's or publick entertainments, probably as punch is in a Puppet show. It was the figure of a man made in basket work 7½ feet high and every [other] way large in proportion, the head was ornamented with four nobs resembling stumps of horns three stood in front and one behind, the whole of this figure was cover'd with feathers, white for the ground upon which [black] imitating hair and the Marks of tattou, it had on a maro or cloth about its loins, under which were proofs of its being intended for the figure of a man.

The differences between this and the earlier description are significant. The 'Monster' has become a 'very extraordinary curiosity'. Cook has learned its name, its purpose and what the white feathers represent and his description is now more precise. Also, though he still does not take it very seriously, he is now prepared to concede that it might be more important than a puppet was for

Europeans. His initial reaction has been modified by what he has learned from careful inquiry. Cook underwent many similar changes of attitude as he assimilated his experiences in Tahiti. He came to the island a practical, scientific man. He left it still a practical, scientific man, but also one who had begun to think about people's lives in society from more than a purely practical or scientific perspective. A strange illumination had begun.

Cook's imaginative growth began in Tahiti, progressed in New Zealand, and reached maturity in Australia. Tahiti was Cook's first experience of the 'unnatural' world, and though there were large and obvious differences between Tahiti and England, and between Europeans and Tahitians, Cook the European was able to find comforting similarities as well, which he brought out in his descriptions. To a lesser extent, he was again able to find similarities in New Zealand. But in Australia, he was hardly able to find them at all. If the Maori and their world were less European than the Tahitians and theirs, then the New Hollanders and their world were so un-European as to seem utterly alien.

Australia presented Cook with the quintessential experience of an 'unnatural' world; and the two months he spent in and around the Endeavour River on its northeastern coast epitomised this experience. As he had followed the often inhospitable coast northwards, Cook had found himself among 'the most dangerous navigation that perhaps ever Ship was in'. From the coastal hills around the Endeavour River he could see only too well the 'Meloncholy prospect of the difficultys we were [to] incounter, for in what ever direction we turn'd our eys Shoals inum[erable] were to be seen'. The fauna and flora of this land, which had been isolated from the rest of the world for millennia, were unique and indescribably un-European. The 'Indians' were alien and mysterious.

Added to the earlier description of these people by William Dampier ('the miserablest People in the World . . . setting aside their Humane Shape, they differ but little from Brutes'), the observations by Cook and Joseph Banks were to form the basis for the British government's 1786 decision to settle 'New South Wales' without negotiating with the Aborigines for land. Cook and Banks saw few people on the coast—never more than '30 or 40 together',

Banks said—and therefore surmised that the vast interior was probably uninhabited. The Aborigines had few material possessions. They
all went completely naked, not using even animal skins to guard
their modesty or protect themselves from the elements. And their
houses were little more than windbreaks. In some areas, Banks
recorded,

*a house was . . . nothing but a hollow shelter about 3 or 4 feet
deep . . . and . . . covered with bark; one side of this was
intirely open which was always that which was sheltered from
the course of the prevailing wind, and opposite to this door
was always a heap of ashes, the remains of a fire probably
more necessary to defend them from Mosquetos than cold.*

To the Europeans, the Aborigines seemed

*never [to] make any stay in [their houses] but wandering like
the Arabs from place to place set them up whenever they meet
with one where sufficient supplys of food are to be met with,
and as soon as these are exhausted remove to another leaving
the houses behind, which are framd with less art or rather
less industry than any habitations of human beings probably
that the world can shew.*

The Aborigines did not grow crops, raise herds and flocks, or
manufacture products. Their few utensils, weapons and ornaments
were crudely fashioned from wood, stone, shell, bark, bone, or hair
to meet only basic needs. Having nothing to trade, the Aborigines
also showed very little interest in the items the Europeans proffered.
The Botany Bay people did not touch the 'Cloth, Looking glasses,
Combs, Beeds Nails &ca' that Cook left for them. The Endeavour
River people showed a similar disdain. As Banks later said, 'there

was nothing we could offer that they would take except provisions and those we wanted ourselves'.

The Aborigines also appeared to have no social, political, or religious organisations as the Europeans understood these. True, they used language (though neither Cook nor Banks nor the Tahitian priest Tupaia, by this time skilled at improvising in situations like this, could at first understand 'one word they said'); and, true, they lived in family groupings. But the voyagers saw no signs of any larger social structures, hierarchies, or political institutions. As Banks later said, he and Cook had no information about the 'Government under which [the Aborigines] lived', nor about their religion. To them and to their contemporaries, the implication was clear—if these people had any social structures at all, they were of the most rudimentary kind.

Cook's and Banks's reports indicated that the Aborigines had attained only the 'first stage' of civilisation, that of

> *a small society whose members live by hunting and fishing, and know only how to make rather crude weapons and household utensils and to build or dig for themselves a place in which to live, [who possess] a language with which to communicate their needs, and a small number of moral ideas which serve as common laws of conduct; [and who live] in families, [and conform] to general customs which take the place of laws.*

Because they did not domesticate animals or cultivate food, and especially because they had no political representatives capable of negotiating on behalf of the whole society, in European eyes the Aborigines had not subdued and cultivated the Earth so as to obtain 'dominion' over it. In the words of John Locke, one of the most influential writers on the laws of nature and nations, New South Wales was one of those

> *great Tracts of Ground . . . which (the Inhabitants thereof not having joyned with the rest of Mankind, in the consent of the*

Use of their common Money) lie waste, and are more than the People, who dwell on it, do, or can make use of, and so still lie in common.

In Cook's words, it was 'in the pure state of Nature, the Industry of Man [having] had nothing to do with any part of it'. To Cook (and to Banks and their contemporaries), eastern New Holland was therefore *terra nullius* (i.e., land *belonging* to no one), to be possessed on the basis of first discovery and effective occupation.

But if he saw the Aborigines in this light, Cook also saw them in less conventional ways. As he experienced the 'unnatural' world he let go of European preconceptions and prejudices. As he did so, he came to the knowledge which was to shape his future. It was knowledge of which he seems to have had little inkling when he left England, and it was knowledge which, finally, transformed him from a good navigator and a fine surveyor into the greatest sailor in the annals of the sea, and into one of the makers of the modern imagination.

As he had entered the Pacific, Cook had hardly been conscious of the scientific marvels Banks and Solander delighted in, writing that these were valuable only because they were unknown in Europe. By the time he left the Pacific, Cook's perspectives had widened so much that he was able to show an intuitive awareness of ethnology as he wondered if the natives of New Holland and New Guinea were once one people. Among the shoals of the Great Barrier Reef, in danger of being swept at any moment against a 'wall of Coral Rock rising all most perpendicular out of the unfathomable Ocean', he had discovered what it was to be an explorer. After the *Endeavour* had narrowly escaped destruction a second time, he wrote: 'Was it not for the pleasure which naturly results to a Man from being the first discoverer, even was it nothing more than sands and Shoals, this service would be insuportable especialy in far distant parts, like this, short of Provisions and almost every other necessary.'

When he turned into Torres Strait, Cook had also arrived at that sense of human community which is the best indication of his imaginative growth and, in the end, of his greatness. He did not reach this point immediately, nor without some help. Before they left England Lord Morton, the President of the Royal Society, had offered him, Banks and Solander some 'Hints', urging them to adopt the 'utmost patience and forbearance' in their dealings with the natives of the lands they would visit. 'They are human creatures,' Morton wrote, 'the work of the same omnipotent Author, equally under his care with the most polished European; perhaps being less offensive, more entitled to his favor.' The Admiralty, too, had instructed the voyagers to show the natives 'every kind of Civility and Regard'.

When they reached Tahiti, Cook drew on Morton's memorandum and issued as his first 'Rule' for their stay, 'To endeavour by every fair means to cultivate a friendship with the Natives and to treat them with all imaginable humanity.' But at first the ideal and the real were not well matched, even in Cook. He was rather offhand about 'the Man who took the Musquet [and] was shott dead before he had got far from the Tent', and his attitude towards the body was less than reverent: 'Yesterday as Mr Green and Dr Munkhouse were taking a Walk they happen'd to meet with the Body of the Man we had Shot, as the Natives by signs made them fully understand, the manner in which the body was enterr'd being a little extraordinary I went to day with some others to see it . . .' But as Cook assimilated the Tahitian experience he became more sensitive; and as the ship ventured farther into the unknown and increasingly strange world of the Pacific, his compassion and understanding grew.

This did not happen without pain and a sense of isolation. Cook had to face, for example, the reality of the murder of the Maori in Poverty Bay. 'I am aware that most humane men who have not experienced things of this nature,' he wrote after this painful event, 'will cencure my conduct in fireing upon the people in this boat nor do I my self think that the reason I had for seizing upon her will att all justify me, and had I thought that they would have made the least resistance I would not have come near them, but as they did I was not to stand still and suffer either my self or those that were with me to be knocked on the head.' By the time Cook left the Pacific, his compassion and understanding had increased so much that he was able to write of the natives of New Holland that, though 'they may appear to some to be the most wretched people upon Earth, . . . in reality they are far more happier than we Europeans; being wholly unacquainted not only with the superfluous but the necessary Conveniences so much sought after in Europe, they are happy in not knowing the use of them.' So when Cook arrived back in England in 1771, he brought with him a sense of the merits of non-European societies, of the variousness of the world, and above all, of his destiny as an explorer.

4

THE GREATEST OF ALL OCEANIC EXPLORATIONS

James Cook's second voyage, 1772–1775

The objective Cook did not achieve on the *Endeavour* voyage was the discovery of *Terra Australis Incognita*. Indeed, by the time he had reached New Zealand, he had come to believe that this continent did not exist. But since there was an area of the southern Pacific (centred on 40°S latitude 140°W longitude) where no European had yet sailed, it was still possible that it did.

Cook returned to England with a fully developed scheme for solving the mystery once and for all:

the most feasable Method of making fu[r]ther discoveries in the
South Sea is to enter it by the way of New Zeland, first
touching and refreshing at the Cape of Good Hope, from thence
proceed to the Southward of New Holland for Queen
Charlottes Sound [in New Zealand] where again refresh Wood
and Water, takeing care to be ready to leave that place by the
latter end of September or beginning of October at farthest,
when you would have the whole summer before you and after
geting through the Straight might, with the prevailing Westerly
winds, run to the Eastward in as high a Latitude as you
please and, if you met with no lands, would have time enough
to get round Cape Horne before the summer was too far spent,
but if after meeting with no Continent & you had other
Objects in View, than haul to the northward and after visiting
some of the Islands already discover'd, after which proceed

with the trade wind back to the Westward in search of those
before Mintioned thus the discoveries in the South Sea would
be compleat.

Carrying out this plan became the fundamental purpose of his second voyage.

Cook sailed in the *Resolution*, together with Tobias Furneaux in the *Adventure*, on 13 July 1772. On board Cook's ship were the scientists Johann Reinhold Forster and his son Georg Forster. He reached Table Bay on 30 October. On leaving it he searched the south Atlantic first, and though Bouvet and Kerguelen had returned from voyaging in this area with reports of a continent, Cook found no evidence of it as he made a cautious way among icebergs and pack ice. He became the first person to cross the Antarctic Circle on 17 January 1773. He lost contact with Furneaux on the way to New Zealand, but this did not worry him since they had already agreed to rendezvous at Queen Charlotte Sound. He sighted New Zealand on 25 March and, after pausing in Dusky Sound, found Furneaux on 18 May 1773. He had sailed for 117 days and 16 000 km without sight of land. Because of the regimen he insisted on, his crew were in good health. He had found no continent.

Cook refreshed the ships in Queen Charlotte Sound, then left on 7 June to search the area of the southern Pacific which he had not sailed through on his previous voyage. It was the last area where the continent, if it existed, might lie. He proceeded east until 15 July, then, in 137°W longitude and having sighted no land, he turned north, to reach Tahiti on 15 August. He was now sure that there was no great continent in the southern hemisphere.

After refreshing his crews and taking on new supplies, Cook sailed again on 1 September, and cruised among the Society Islands, the Cook Islands, and the Friendly Islands in September and early October. He sighted New Zealand again on 21 October, and reached Queen Charlotte Sound on 3 November without Furneaux, having lost him in stormy weather off Cape Campbell. The weather delayed Furneaux from reaching the rendezvous at Ship Cove, and by the time he did so Cook had gone. As he prepared to sail again, he sent a party of ten men ashore to cut greens, whom the Maori killed and ate, much to the horror of those on board the ship. With the *Adventure* in poor condition and running short of provisions, Furneaux sailed across the southern Pacific and Atlantic to the Cape of Good Hope, then on to England, which he reached in mid-July 1774. With him went Omai (Mai), a young man from Huahine, who was to startle the English social world with his innate grace, and inspire some of its members with dreams of a life in the state of nature.

When Furneaux missed their rendezvous, Cook left him a message sealed in a bottle, then sailed for a second sweep across the southern Pacific on 24 November. He crossed the Antarctic Circle for the second time on 21 December, and was then forced to turn north by the intense cold and thick pack ice. He held a northerly course until 11 January 1774, when he once again swung south. On 26 January he crossed the Antarctic Circle for the third time, and by 30 January he had reached 71°10' S latitude. He was now only 200 km from the coast of Antarctica and, faced with an impassable ice field, he thought he had gone as far as man could go. He had found no continent in his great sweeps across the southern Atlantic and Pacific Oceans, and he had therefore 'intirely refuted' the 'assertions and conjectures' of those who had written about *Terra Australis*. As he turned north once more, he ended his and his nation's search for the southern continent.

Now that he had resolved 'this thing which at times has been the object of many ages and Nations', he was free to pursue other interests, and he decided to cross the Pacific by following in Quirós's path. He reached Easter Island on 11 March 1774, Mendaña's Marquesas Islands on 7 April, and Tahiti on 21 April. He left Tahiti again on 14 May, sighted Tonga on 26 June and the first island of Quirós's Austrialia del Espiritu Santo on 17 July. Cook renamed the group the New Hebrides. He sailed among these islands in July and August, anchoring on 25 August in the bay which Quirós had named in honour of St Philip and St James in 1606. From Espiritu Santo, the largest of the group, he sailed southwest, discovering New Caledonia on 4 September. He edged along its shoal-fringed eastern coast until 1 October, nearly losing the *Resolution* on reefs on

Capt.ᵗ James Cook
of the Endeavour.

Portrait of Cook, William Hodges (1776), courtesy of the National Maritime Museum, Greenwich

Evidently painted about the time of Cook's return to England at the conclusion of his second voyage in 1776, Hodges's depiction well conveys the explorer's driven personality (and perhaps also his ill-health!).

Review of the War Galleys at Tahiti, William Hodges (c.1775–6), courtesy of the National Maritime Museum, Greenwich

In an extraordinary gesture, at Pare at the end of April 1774, the admiral-priests showed Cook that Tahitians were also men of the sea, by marshalling approximately 160 double-hulled war canoes, and some 170 smaller canoes, together carrying approximately 8000 men. Cook wrote, 'the whole made a grand and Noble appearance such as was never seen before in this Sea'.

Tahiti Revisited, William Hodges (c.1776), courtesy of the National Maritime Museum, Greenwich

With its lushness, climate and sensual ambience, the Europeans found Tahiti to be a garden of earthly delight. But there were darker aspects of Tahitian life, whose presence Hodges—perhaps unknowingly—conveyed when he depicted the *tii* figure watching over the bathing girls.

An offering before Capt Cook, John Webber, courtesy of the Mitchell Library, SLNSW

The Hawaiians took Captain Cook to be an incarnation of the god Lono, visiting in the proper time of the *makahiki*. As such, it was necessary to greet him in the appropriate ceremonial ways. Webber depicted Cook seated on a dais, with Lono's iconography behind him, receiving the offerings of the priests of Lono's temple at Kealakekua Bay.

The Landing at Mallicolo, William Hodges (1774), courtesy of the National Maritime Museum, Greenwich

Apart from its ethnographic details, this painting is interesting because it shows the method Cook developed for meeting indigenous people. He is shown putting aside his musket, and reaching out for the proffered green branch.

Mrs Elizabeth Cook, aged 81 years, W. Henderson (1830), courtesy of the Mitchell Library, SLNSW

Mrs Cook outlived her explorer husband by many years. Before she died, she is reported to have destroyed all his letters to her. It would be good to know something more of her life and perceptions, particularly of the world that James Cook has so much altered.

The Death of Captain Cook, John Webber, courtesy of the Dixson Galleries, SLNSW

Webber strikingly depicts the tumult as the rocky spit that formed the edge of both land and sea at Kealakekua Bay on 14 February 1779, when Cook was struck down. What did Cook's gesture in reaching out to the marines in the waiting boats mean? Was he telling them to come into shore? or to stop firing? or to push off?

16 and 28 September. Then, continuing southwards, he discovered Norfolk Island on 10 October and reached Queen Charlotte Sound on 18 October.

Leaving again, refreshed, on 9 November, Cook crossed the Pacific between 50°S and 55°S latitude and thus completed the exploration of its southern reaches. By the end of the month he had given up hope of finding extensive land. He reached the western entrance of the Straits of Magellan on 17 December, spent two weeks making observations on the coastline of Tierra del Fuego, and set out into the south Atlantic on 4 January 1775. While he found some small islands, he again found no continent, nor any signs of one, in a navigable latitude. He speculated that if there was a continent, it must lie within the Antarctic Circle. Knowing how foolish it would be to risk 'all which had been done in the Voyage' on investigating that possibility, he turned for home on 6 February. He reached Cape Town on 21 March, Ascension Island on 28 May, and anchored at Spithead on 30 July. He had been away three years and eighteen days, had sailed more than 110 000 km and had lost only four of his crew. He had shown that there was no *Terra Australis Incognita*, unless it lay around the South Pole, where 'no man will ever venture'.

There are good reasons for seeing Cook's second voyage as the greatest of all oceanic explorations. In that voyage he determinedly carried out a skilful plan and demonstrated once and for all that the long-dreamed-of southern continent did not exist. He made successful use of John Harrison and Larcum Kendall's chronometer, which, by allowing navigators to measure elapsed time, greatly simplified the calculation of longitude at sea. He kept the *Resolution*'s crew healthy. The scientists on board brought back splendid natural history collections, and made a pioneering attempt at determining global weather patterns. They (and Cook) also recorded much valuable ethnographic information, of which perhaps the most striking was Cook's description of the spectacle at Pare, Tahiti, in April 1774, when the admiral-priests paraded their fleet of 160 war canoes before the Europeans. 'Their Vessels were decorated with Flags, Streamers &ca,' wrote Cook, 'so that the whole made a grand and Noble appearance such as was never seen before in this Sea.'

Behind all these accomplishments stands the brooding figure of Cook himself, the skilled and humane explorer of the sea at the height of his powers. Now knowing that his ambition was to go 'not only further than any other man has been before me, but as far as I think it possible for man to go', he also knew what lay before him. As he prepared to leave the Cape of Good Hope to pioneer a new route to the Pacific, he wrote to his old master and friend John Walker:

Having nothing new to communicate I should hardly have troubled you with a letter was it not customary for Men to take leave of their friends before they go out of the World, for I can hardly think my self in it so long as I am deprived from having any Connections with the civilized part of it, and this will soon be my case for two years at least. When I think of the Inhospitable parts I am going to, I think the Voyage dangerous, I however enter upon it with great cheerfullness, Providence has been very kind to me on many occasions and I trust in the continuation of the divine protection; I have two good Ships well provided and well Man'd.

Cook's pursuit of his ambition produced a great rhythm in his second voyage—an oscillation between massive sweeps across the reaches of ocean, and periods of quietude resting and refreshing at the tropical islands; between unremitting struggle in the weird Antarctic—with its phantasmagorical southern lights and its eerie silences broken by the sounds of crumbling ice and sounding whales—and the warm, lush, erotic, life-restoring ambience of Polynesia. Cook wrote of 24 December 1773, when the *Resolution* was in 67°S latitude,

[we] made sail to the westward under double reef'd Top-sails and Courses, with the wind no[r]therly a strong gale attended

with a thick fog Sleet and Snow which froze to the Rigging as it fell and decorated the whole with icicles. Our ropes were like wires, Sails like board or plates of Metal and the Shivers froze fast in the blocks so that it required our utmost effort to get a Top-sail down and up; the cold so intense as hardly to be endured, the whole Sea in a manner covered with ice, a hard gale and a thick fog.

And of the *Resolution's* arrival at Tahiti, the scientist Georg Forster wrote:

It was one of those beautiful mornings which the poets of all nations have attempted to describe, when we saw the isle of O-Taheite, within two miles before us. The east-wind which had carried us so far, was entirely vanished, and a faint breeze only wafted a delicious perfume from the land, and curled the surface of the sea.

Cook moved about the world he had made his own with great assurance, and not only because of his seamanship. When he left the Pacific on his first voyage, he had come to see that European reality was not the only one, nor even in certain circumstances the most appropriate one. Understanding this, and acknowledging how much he depended on indigenous peoples for the success of this voyage, he developed a set procedure. As one of his officers described it:

no man could be better calculated to gain the confidence of Savages than Capt. Cook. He was brave, uncommonly Cool, Humane, and Patient. He would land alone unarmed, or lay aside his Arms, and sit down when they threatened with theirs, throwing them Beads, Knives, and other little presents, then by

55

degrees advancing nearer, till by patience and forbearance, he gained their friendship and an intercourse with them, which to people in our situation was of the utmost consequence.

This attitude underpinned Cook's actions on the second voyage. On his return to Tahiti, for example, an old woman told him tearfully of the death of her son:

she seized me by both hands and burst into a flood of tears saying Toutaha Tiyo no Toute matte (Toutaha the friend of Cook is dead). I was so much affected at her behavour that it would not have been possible for me to refrain mingling tears with hers had not Otoo come and snatched me as it were from her.

This empathetic man was a new Cook—one who was able to move so far beyond the borders of European culture that he could exchange names with the ruling chief of Huahine and understand fully all the rights and obligations involved in that exchange. When, in September 1773, Cook's officers were assaulted and had their weapons and clothes stolen, Oree (the chief's title)—much against his people's wishes—voluntarily placed himself in Cook's power as insurance for the items' return. This gesture, Cook wrote:

in a great degree shews that Friendship is Sacred with these people. Oree and I were profess'd friends in all the forms customary among them and he had no idea that this could be broke by the act of any other person, indeed this seem'd to be the great Argument he made use of to his people when they opposed his going into my boat, his words were to this effect: Oree (for so I was always call'd) and I are friends, I have done nothing to forfeit his friendship, why should I not go with him.

❧ VIEWS OF THE PALE-SKINNED STRANGERS ❧

Much has been written about how Europeans 'viewed' the peoples they encountered in and about the Pacific Ocean. But how did the Pacific peoples view the interlopers? After all, the arrival of a comparatively large sailing vessel carrying some 100 men must have been at least surprising, if not threatening. We now know that the Natives of Tahiti initially viewed the Strangers of the *Dolphin* as manifestations or representatives of the god 'Oro; and that the Natives of Hawaii took Cook to be a manifestation of the god Lono.

But how did the Maori of New Zealand, the Aborigines of Australia, the Melanesians of the Western Pacific, or the peoples of the northwest Pacific coast view the Europeans? This question is difficult to answer, for none of the indigenous cultures kept written records; oral traditions are sparse and most are untrustworthy in important ways; and the European records inevitably interpret events from European points of view.

Still, we can offer some answers. The Maori may not have accorded godly status to Europeans in the same way the Tahitians and Hawaiians did, but at least initially, they too regarded them as supernatural beings—*tupua* ('goblins'). Anne Salmond has pointed out that the way in which the Maori met Tasman's expedition, with ritual incantations and sounding from shell trumpets, paralleled the way in which they usually repelled spirits at night.

Late in life, Horeta Te Taniwha, who had seen it as a child, recorded the appearance of the *Endeavour* at Whitianga Harbour in November 1769.

[W]hen our old men saw the ship they said it was an atua, a god, and the people on board were tupua, strange beings or 'goblins'. The ship came to anchor, and the boats pulled on shore. As our old men looked at the manner in which they came on shore, the rowers pulling with their backs to the bows of the boat, the old people said, 'Yes, it is so: these people are goblins; their eyes are at the back of their heads; they pull on shore with their backs to the land to which they are going.' When these goblins came on shore we (the children and women) took notice of them, but we ran away from them into the forest, and the warriors alone stayed in the presence of those goblins; but as the goblins stayed some time, and did not do any evil to our braves, we came back one by one, and gazed at them, and we stroked their garments with our hands, and we were pleased with the whiteness of their

skins and the blue of the eyes of some of them.

Clearly, though, this awe did not last very long. Repeatedly, Maori fought to repel the Strangers. And seeing that the light-skinned Strangers could be killed (as well as that they desired women), the Maori would have quickly concluded that they too were human.

The peoples of the western Pacific, if they ever saw the Strangers as supernatural beings, seem to have very quickly abandoned the idea, and come to regard them as meddlesome humans with a disturbing penchant for violating *tapu* (taboo). When among the Santa Cruz Islands in August 1767, Carteret sent a boat party inshore to find a safe anchorage for the ship. Contrary to orders, the master landed and had his men get some coconuts by cutting down a tree. He then

found himself attacked by a great Number of Canoes by sea and (as they say) some hundreds of men by land, from all which he was glad to get off, himself and half the boats Crew wounded of which wounds he and three of them died aftrwards.

To people to whom good gardens are necessary to propitiate the ancestral spirits and ward off evil, the wanton felling of a coconut tree must have seemed a grave offence indeed.

The peoples of the northwest Pacific coast also possessed cultures informed by magical conceptions of the world. The Tlingit people, for example, initially supposed that Lapérouse's people were servants of Yehlh, the spirit who created birds. However, their own well-established trading habits certainly helped the west coast Natives to incorporate the Russians, English, French and Spanish into their economic network. And the more familiar the ways of the Strangers, the more human they were likely to seem.

Knowing how the Australian Aborigines viewed the Europeans is

And when Cook, farewelling the ruling chief of Raiatea, was asked for the name of his *marae*, he was able to make the appropriate reply: 'Stepney', the name of his London parish.

Well before most Europeans of his era, Cook had come to understand the relativity of cultural values. Now he was able to watch impartially a Maori eat human flesh so as to confirm the most problematic of all, partly because of the paucity of the sources, and partly because it may be quite misleading to generalise over the whole continent and several centuries on the basis of the response at a particular place and time.

At least initially, Aborigines tended to avoid contact with the Strangers. Cook wrote of how, at Botany Bay, 'The strings of beeds &ca we had left with the children last night were found laying in the hut this morning'. Part of the reason for their shyness was no doubt fear. On their first landing, Cook wrote, '[Men, women and children] all made off except two men who seemd resolved to oppose our landing'. Later, a strolling midshipman offered 'a very old man and woman and two small Children' a bird he had shot, 'which they would not touch neither did they speak one word but seem'd to be much frighten'd'.

Records of culture contact in the nineteenth century show that a common Aboriginal response was to view the light-skinned Strangers as returning spirits of dead Aborigines, who might be incorporated into the family or group if recognised, but who if unrecognised remained sinister. If this is how the Botany Bay people viewed the Strangers, it would explain their apprehension, and their reluctance to pick up goods imbued with another being's spirit. Some Aborigines at least certainly saw Cook's presence on the eastern coast in 1770 as a manifestation of the supernatural. When the people of Fraser Island saw the *Endeavour* pass north towards what they called Thoorvour and Cook named Breaksea Spit, they incorporated the event into their cosmology:

These strangers, where are they going?
Where are they trying to steer?
They must be in that place, Thoorvour,
it is true.
See the smoke coming in from the sea.
These men must be burying themselves
like the sand crabs.
They disappeared like the smoke.

existence of a practice Europeans considered so inhuman as to be impossible. Referring to those learned men who had doubted his reports of cannibalism after his first voyage, he remarked that 'few considers what a savage man is in his original state', and wondered how deep the influence of cultural norms really went.

Now, he was fully conscious of how European explorers must appear to islanders. Of Tana in the New Hebrides he wrote:

> its impossible for them to know our real design, we enter their Ports without their daring to make opposition, we attempt to land in a peaceable manner, if this succeeds its well, if not we land nevertheless and mentain the footing we thus got by the Superiority of our fire arms, in what other light can they then at first look upon us but as invaders of their Country.

He knew, too, what devastation contact with alien cultures wreaked. Noticing that prostitution was greatly increased during his second visit to Queen Charlotte Sound in June 1773, he observed:

> now we find the men are the chief promoters of this Vice, and for a spike nail or any other thing they value will oblige their Wives and Daughters to prostitute themselves whether they will or no and that not with the privicy decency seems to require, such are the concequences of a commerce with Europeans and what is still more to our Shame civilized Christians, we debauch their Morals already too prone to vice and we interduce among them wants and perhaps diseases which they never before knew and which serves only to disturb the happy tranquillity they and their fore Fathers had injoy'd.

Cook tried as hard as he could to limit the damage, asking and paying for food, water and wood, and punishing crewmen who had sex with native women while carrying venereal infections.

Of course there were moments of particular failure; but on the whole Cook was so successful in his dealings with the islanders that an unusual humanity permeated the second voyage. As he prepared to leave Tahiti in May 1774, having ended his search for the southern continent and knowing he might not come again, the sailors encouraged some Tahitians to sail with them, holding out prospects of wealth. One young native was more persistent than all the rest. 'I thought it proper to undeceive him,' Cook wrote,

thinking it an Act of the highest injustice to take away a person from these isles against his own free inclination under any promise whatever much more that of bringing them back again . . . which was not in my power to perform.

When Cook sailed from Huahine, the old chief they called Oree was the last Polynesian to leave the ship. '[W]hen he took leave I told him we should see each other no more[,] at which he wept saying than let your sons come we will treat them well.' Cook the humane European could have received no greater tribute.

Cook was also a dauntless explorer and indefatigable recorder of scientific detail. He was the first person to cross the Antarctic Circle, and it would be another 100 years before anyone went farther than his 71°S latitude. He discovered the Friendly Islands, New Caledonia and Norfolk Island, and rediscovered the Marquesas and the New Hebrides groups. Always, he charted, recorded, and asked questions.

Cook gained the achievements of the second voyage in the face of many dangers. On some moonless nights in August 1773, he appeared unexpectedly on deck to order changes in direction that avoided unseen shoals. Then, at Tahiti, when working into Vaitepetia Bay, he saved both ships from wreck after a desperate struggle. In the wastes of the southern ocean in December 1773 and January 1774, he avoided both striking the numerous icebergs and being trapped by pack ice. At Eromanga in the New Hebrides in August 1774, his instinct suddenly told him that the welcoming Melanesians intended to slaughter him and his boat's crew, and he was able to pull off to safety. At New Caledonia the following month, he found the *Resolution* in the same dreadful circumstances as the *Endeavour* had faced in August 1770, with no wind, in deep water, and being swept towards a reef by a massive swell. Once more, he somehow avoided disaster.

Cook's skill and intuition were perhaps no more than the result of his long experience of oceans, islands and people. But in the desolate expanses of the Pacific, to his crew he seemed something more than human in his management of circumstance, and they followed him devotedly. Of the 90 seamen aboard the *Resolution*, seventeen had been with Cook on the *Endeavour*; and several of this second-voyage crew would rejoin him on the third. 'He was beloved by his people, who looked up to him as a father, and obeyed his commands with alacrity,' one companion wrote. 'The confidence we placed in him was unremitting; our admiration for his great talents unbounded.' Showing themselves 'capable of surmounting every difficulty and danger which came in their way', this crew also won Cook's praise. And he brought almost all of them safely home: 'On Saturday the 29 [July 1775] we made the land near Plymouth and the next morning anchored at Spit-head. Having been absent from England Three Years and Eighteen Days, in which time I lost but four men and one only of them by sickness.'

It is impossible not to see the Cook of the second voyage as an embodiment of the mythic hero who ventures into the underworld and emerges triumphant from it. In the records of this voyage, and in the European imagination, the repeated swings between island and ocean are also swings between heaven and hell. The island where the hero moves about in peace and harmony is cosmos; the reef, or the frozen waste of ocean that threatens destruction, is chaos. And, as in the mythic stories, the passage from the known to the unknown world and back restores life and validates experience. In James Cook of the second voyage—navigator, explorer, geographer, ethnographer, archetypal voyager—the Europeans of the Enlightenment found a new hero, whose brooding intensity William Hodges's 1776 portrait captures so well.

5

AN EVER-DARKENING ASPECT

James Cook's third voyage, 1776–1780

At the same time as Cook was removing the last possibilities that *Terra Australis* existed, people in England were pressing for a northern passage to be found from the Atlantic to the Pacific Ocean. At the urging of Daines Barrington, in January 1773 the Royal Society asked Lord Sandwich to send a ship to explore the Arctic Ocean, which, by a serious error of reasoning, was thought to be ice-free. Banks's friend Constantine John Phipps (later Lord Mulgrave) set off that summer, only to encounter impassable pack ice north of Spitzbergen.

The next year, Barrington and the Royal Society took up the matter again, this time arguing for an approach from the west (i.e., from the northeast Pacific); and after some discussion Sandwich agreed to authorise such an expedition once Cook had returned from his second voyage. In 1775 Barrington persuaded Parliament to make the commanders of Royal Navy ships eligible for the £20 000 reward for finding the elusive passage, and to extend the geographical limits within which it was to be found. Barrington's scheme became the basis of Cook's third voyage. Historians have tended to view this voyage, as they have the first and second ones, as chiefly a scientific expedition, but this neglects the full picture. The suggestion that a search for the passage be mounted from the west was based not only on geographical curiosity but on commercial ambitions. And it seems the original idea was not Barrington's alone.

In 1758–59, serving on Captain Edward Hughes's ship *Somerset*, John Blankett participated in the campaigns against the French in Louisbourg and Quebec. There, according to the author of an 1802 memoir in the *Gentleman's Magazine*, who said he had known Blankett for over 30 years, the young man began to speculate about the existence of a Northwest Passage and evidently presented a memorandum on the subject to the Admiralty. In 1774, Blankett, now a lieutenant, asked the Admiralty to let him travel to Holland and Russia, with the aim of gathering further information about Dutch discoveries in the seas around Korea and Japan, and about Russian discoveries on the northeast coast of Asia and in the northern Pacific. Informing Blankett that his request would be granted, Sandwich cautioned:

> *I must beg to repeat to you that anything that has passed between you and me is to be considered as [not] binding me in the most distant engagement, either to undertake a voyage of discovery to the Northwest of America; or (if such a voyage shou'd be undertaken) to the appointment of any of the Officers to be employed on such [an] expedition: and your voyage to Petersbourg must be understood as merely your own act in search of knowledge & information, without being founded on any particular advice or encouragement from me.*

Unfortunately, our knowledge of Blankett's mission remains extremely sketchy. But he clearly found some interesting information, for when he returned at the end of 1774 he gave Sandwich a memorandum (now lost) dealing with the Russian discoveries, and a nineteen-page account of 'Seas of Japan'. In this second paper, after giving details of reported voyages from Asia and Europe to the northwest American coast, Blankett described the Liu Kiu [Ryukyu] Islands, and suggested that Britain should begin a trade with their inhabitants so as 'to introduce a new vent for our Manufactures & [to increase] the Naval power of the Nation'. On an accompanying map, he showed the coasts and islands of East Asia, and some of the Russian discoveries in the Aleutian Islands and on the coast of America. In March 1775 Blankett gave Sandwich another memorandum, this time dealing with Spanish penetration of New Mexico, and also repeating the likely advantages of establishing a factory on the Liu Kiu Islands.

Later, Blankett claimed that there was an intimate connection between his ideas and the objectives of Cook's third voyage. He said not only that he had consulted Dr John Campbell and drawn up a proposal for a 'voyage of Discovery', which was in fact that which Barrington put before the Council of the Royal Society in February 1774; but also that the idea of opening trade with northern Asia 'made a part of the Plan submitted by me to Lord Sandwich in 1773 [1774?] and [was] by him [engrafted?] on Captain Cook's last Voyage but frustrated by his death'. Unfortunately, there is no independent evidence to confirm these claims, but Blankett's contact with Sandwich gives them some plausibility. If so, then we have to consider that there were commercial as well as scientific motives behind Cook's third voyage.

On his return in 1776, Cook was received with high honours. The Admiralty promoted him to Post-Captain and appointed him to a well-paid position at Greenwich Hospital for disabled sailors, a prestigious job and a comfortable sinecure for a man without wealth, social or political power and of comparatively junior rank; and the Royal Society elected him a Fellow. Cook spent the autumn and winter preparing a book on his second voyage and mingling with London's high and literary society.

Within days of his return, it became clear that the Admiralty would indeed mount a third voyage of Pacific exploration. It also became clear, at least to his friends, that Cook was ambivalent about staying put. As he told John Walker on 19 August: 'a few Months ago the whole Southern hemisphere was hardly enough for me and now I am going to be confined within the limits of Greenwich Hospital, which are far too small for an active mind like mine . . . I must however confess it is a fine retreat and a pretty income, but whether I can bring my self to like ease and retirement, time will shew.' It was a restlessness his admiring patrons found it all too easy to play upon. Early in February 1776, Lord Sandwich reportedly invited Cook, Admiral Palliser and Admiralty Secretary Philip Stephens to dine with him so as to discuss the forthcoming voyage.

After John Webber, The Inside of House at Nootka Sound
Many of the exploring expeditions carried artists, whose task it was to help record scientific and ethnographic detail. This engraving depicts many details of the Nootka's domestic and cultural life, and is therefore a valuable ethnographic addition to the officers' written descriptions.

Cook, his contemporary biographer wrote, was 'so fired with the contemplation and representation of the object, that he started up and declared that he himself would undertake the direction of the enterprise'.

Cook sailed in the *Resolution* on 12 July 1776, and three months later reached Table Bay, where he was joined by Charles Clerke in the *Discovery*. The two ships sailed again on 1 December. They sighted Prince Edward, Crozet, and Kerguelen Islands on their way to Van Diemen's Land, which they reached on 24 January 1777. Cook then crossed to New Zealand and refreshed at Queen Charlotte Sound. He sailed around the Cook Islands in March and April, and spent May, June and July among the Tongan islands. He sighted Tahiti again on 12 July, refreshed, and left on 29 September. He sailed among the Society Islands until 11 December, when he turned north for the North American coast. After spending Christmas at

Christmas Island, he discovered the Hawaiian Islands on 18 January 1778. He left these islands on 2 February, to sight the 'long looked for Coast of new Albion [northern California]' on 6 March.

As he followed the American coast north, Cook looked for the 'pretended *Strait of Juan de Fuca*' but did not find it. After spending a month in Nootka Sound, on Vancouver Island, where he repaired the ships, on 26 April he resumed his careful search for a Northwest Passage. He sailed along the Alaskan coast, examining its inlets, islands and passages, and on 8 August entered Bering Strait off Cape Prince of Wales, 'the Western extremity of all America hitherto known'. For the next ten days he sailed north into the Arctic Ocean, then, faced with impassable ice, turned southwest until he reached the Asian coast. On 2 September, having re-entered Bering Strait, the ships passed Cape Dezhneva, the easternmost point of Asia. Cook had found no passage, and as winter was coming on he decided to return to the Hawaiian Islands and continue the search the following summer. After a three-week stop at Unalaska Island, where he replenished supplies, made some repairs, and discussed the coast with some Russian traders, he reached Hawaii at the end of November.

Cook spent the next six weeks cruising around the islands and at the end of January refreshed and repaired the ships in Kealakekua Bay. He left this bay on 4 February, but storms then damaged the *Resolution* and forced him to return. Relations between the Europeans and the Hawaiians quickly deteriorated, and Cook was killed in a fracas on 14 February 1779. Charles Clerke, now the senior officer, took the *Resolution* and *Discovery* out from Kealakekua Bay a week later. They reached the coast of Kamchatka in late April, and in the summer they explored the coast of Asia up to, and through, Bering Strait. Ill with tuberculosis, Clerke died in August, and Captains John Gore and James King then decided to terminate the voyage. They went through the Kurile Islands down past Japan to Macau, where some of the crew sold very profitably the sea-otter pelts they had bartered at Nootka Sound. Leaving in mid-January 1780, the ships reached England again in early October, having been away more than four years.

On the face of things, the third voyage was the equal of the

After John Webber, A Human Sacrifice, in a Morai, in Otaheite
Cook's innate curiosity together with his scientific outlook led him to investigate some aspects of Pacific cultures, such as infanticide, cannibalism and human sacrifice, that many people would find repugnant. That he did so is a mark of how much he was able to suspend conventional judgments in the interest of learning more about the cultures he encountered.

earlier ones. The explorations were as extensive, the charting as thorough as on those voyages; and once more a large geographical misconception was cast into doubt. Extensive natural history collections were again made, and much ethnographical detail obtained about the peoples of the northern Pacific. And Cook once more demonstrated both his humanity and his ability to move beyond the confines of his culture. In New Zealand, for example, he refused to act against Kahura, the Maori who three years before had led the attack on the *Adventure* crewmen which resulted in their death and roasting. When the ships arrived in Queen Charlotte Sound in February 1777, this chief made wary contact, and many (including other Maori) urged Cook to punish him. But 'I admired his courage,' he wrote,

> *and was not a little pleased at the confidence he put in me.*
> *Perhaps in this he put his whole safety, for I had always*
> *declared to those who solicited his death that I had always*
> *been a friend to them all and would continue so unless they*
> *gave me cause to act otherwise; as to what was past, I should*
> *think no more of it as it was some time sence and done when I*

*was not there, but if ever they made a Second attempt of that
kind, they might rest assured of feeling the weight of
my resentment.*

At Tonga, Cook stripped to the waist and loosened his hair so he might witness the '*inasi*. Some of his officers objected, but to the benefit of history Cook ignored them, for his description of this harvest festival remains the best we have. At Tahiti, he agreed to attend a ceremony of human sacrifice, and despite his personal repugnance recorded the details with his usual objectivity.

Yet, as it proceeded, the voyage took on an increasingly dark aspect. Cook fell into wild rages with his crew. At Nootka Sound, for example, he took the midshipman James Trevenen to task over some astronomical observations. 'Of course I had a *heiva* of the old boy,' Trevenen recorded, and explained: '*Heiva* [is] the name of the dances of the Southern Islanders, which bore so great a resemblance to the violent motions and stampings on the Deck of Capt. Cooke in the paroxysms of passion, into which he often threw himself upon the slightest occasion.' In December 1778, Cook flogged the cooper for emptying a cask of 'sugar cane beer' the crew refused to drink. Throughout the voyage, he flogged seamen for theft, for allowing their metal tools to be stolen, for transmitting venereal infections. Yet this harsh regimen brought little change. In the end, Cook wrote exasperatedly of his 'mutinous turbulent crew', and flogged harder.

The thieving by the Melanesians and Polynesians also drove Cook to distraction, and he turned to increasingly vicious methods of punishment. In May 1777, in the Friendly Islands, he flogged an inhabitant of Nomuka caught stealing a piece of iron, and forced him to offer a pig in reparation. A few weeks later at Tonga, he not only flogged thieves and stone throwers, but also slashed their arms. When such measures did not control the stealing and the interference with his working parties, Cook smashed canoes, burnt huts, took chiefs hostage. In October 1777, he led an armed party across Moorea, in the Society Islands, in search of a stolen goat, and burnt and smashed to emphasise his determination to have it back. Thankfully, Cook still refrained from indiscriminate revenge and slaughter, forbidding his sentries to load their muskets with ball. Indeed, one of his officers thought that he 'ever acted with the utmost Impartiality, being as ready to hear the Complaint of an Indian and to see justice done to him when injured, as he was to any of his own Men'. This may have been so, but nonetheless there was on the third voyage a stridency and desperateness to Cook's management of people and events that were absent from the earlier voyages.

There are some obvious reasons for this. Since the third voyage was based on the false assumption that there should be an ice-free northern passage from the Atlantic to the Pacific, it was inevitable that Cook would fail in his quest; and failure in matters of exploration was something he was quite unaccustomed to. Also, Sir James Watt has concluded that on the third voyage Cook may have been suffering severely from roundworm infection of the intestine, and perhaps also from tuberculosis; and he thinks illness goes a long way towards explaining the changes in Cook's character. This is an interesting idea, but there is another possible explanation as well.

The James Cook who returned to England after the second voyage was a man at the height of all his powers, 'who [had] not only made the most extensive, but the most instructive voyages; who [had] not only discovered, but surveyed, vast tracts of new coasts; who [had] dispelled the illusion of a *terra australis incognita*, and fixed the bounds of the habitable earth, as well as those of the navigable ocean, in the southern hemisphere'. This Cook had every reason to consider himself master of the vast Pacific, acquainted with all its aspects, equal to all its challenges. The Pacific Ocean constituted his world; he moved about it easily; he had seen more of it, and knew it better, than any European before him. But there was more to it than that. By the end of the second voyage, Cook had, I think, come to believe that he could control the events of his world as a magician might. If we put aside sheer foolhardiness (which is the opposite to his normal, deliberate character), how else may we explain that daring gesture in January 1774 when, having twice been stopped by ice within the Antarctic Circle, he turned the *Resolution* south again and headed for the Pole? How else may we explain his insistence, against informed advice, on eating a poisonous fish in New Caledonia in September 1774?

We hinted this circumstance to captain Cook, especially as the ugly shape, and large head of the fish, were greatly in its disfavour; but he told us he had eaten this identical sort of fish on the coast of New Holland, during his former voyage, without the least bad consequences.

We can see the same confidence in his ability to master chaos in Cook's account of stepping ashore at Eromanga in the New Hebrides:

I landed in the face of a great Multitude with nothing but a green branch in my hand I had got from of them, I was received very courteously and upon their pressing near the boat, retired upon my makeing Signs to keep off, one Man who seem'd to [be] a Chief a Mongest them at once comprehending what I meant, made them form a kind of Semicircle round the bow of the boat and beat any one who broke through this order.

It was his sense of his explorer's destiny, together with pride in the mastery it had given rise to, that made it impossible for Cook to refuse command of the third voyage. The Pacific was his world; he could not relinquish it to anyone else. But this time, the principles and procedures which had previously enabled him to master it were repeatedly violated. Cook's increasingly desperate actions suggest that, as well as being exhausted and ill, he sensed he was losing his mastery, and falling into chaos.

The fates held off until Hawaii, where the great drama of this singular man's life reached its terrible catharsis. Cook arrived at Kealakekua Bay in the season of Lono, god of peace and fertility. His ships, with their masts, spars and sails, reflected Lono's iconography, and his clockwise progress around the island mirrored Lono's during his annual visitation. The Hawaiians therefore welcomed Cook as an incarnation of this deity, setting him on a throne, draping him with sacred cloths, presenting him with offerings of food. As one of his companions wrote, the 'remarkable homage' paid by the Hawaiians 'on the first visit of Captn. Cook to their houses seemd to approach to Adoration, he was placed at the foot of a wooden image at the Entrance of a hut, to which from the remnants of Cloth round the trunk, & the remains of Offerings on the Whatta, they seem to pay more than ordinary devotion'. Though he did not fully understand what was going on, Cook did sense that the Hawaiians were treating him as more than human; and he went along with this, not only fulfilling their ritual needs, but also confirming his view of himself. When Cook sailed from Kealakekua Bay on 4 February 1779, he did so at the proper time. The rainy season was ending and the harvest, on which the Europeans had placed a great strain, was over. When Cook returned to the bay on 11 February with a cracked mainmast, the Hawaiians' reality was different. It was now the season of Lono's opposite, Ku, the god of war and human sacrifice.

The drama quickly reached its inevitable climax. The Hawaiians showed their resentment of the inappropriate god's requests for food and help by withholding labour, throwing stones, stealing tools, and gathering in large, uneasy crowds. In turn, Cook tried to get his way with ever-greater ferocity, now instructing his sentries to load their muskets with ball. During the night of 13 February, Hawaiians stole the *Discovery's* cutter. The next morning, Cook sent parties in search of it and landed to take a chief hostage, a measure that had previously succeeded in getting stolen goods returned. He was met by 'a numerous and tumultuous body of natives', who were even further inflamed by news that a chief had been murdered along the bay. Cook found his hostage readily enough, the paramount chief Kalani'opu'u, personification of Ku, but as they prepared to step into the boat the chief's followers objected. Cook fired at one Hawaiian who brandished a spear at him. Several others then threw stones, and the marines fired into the crowd of warriors who surged forward. In the chaos, Cook made one last attempt to regain control. Just before he was clubbed down and stabbed, he ordered the marines in the boats offshore to cease their fire. To partake of Lono's *mana*, the Hawaiians hacked Cook's body to pieces, stripped the bones of their flesh, and kept the long ones as sacred relics. After negotiation, the Europeans finally obtained some remnants to bury at sea.

6
IMPERIAL RIVALRIES

A maritime agenda in the Pacific Ocean, 1770–1794

The British explorations, particularly
Cook's, gave an enormous boost to
European imperialism by providing
new possibilities for commercial
expansion—as Manuel de Amat y
Jumient, the Viceroy of Peru, percep-
tively wrote about Wallis's voyage:

*The English, as a necessary
consequence of their interests
and the maxims of their Government, must be keen to establish
themselves at some of the many positions that command the
South Sea . . . it would seem likely that the vessels spoken of
have been despatched . . . with the actual and simple object of
selecting and surveying the most convenient site for a Colony
where they may foster the uses and advantages they have in
view, in time of peace as well as in time of war.*

The British explorations effectively set an agenda which France
and Spain had to follow if they were to remain Britain's imperial
rivals. The Spanish began to do this from the beginning of the
1770s. Thinking, as the French navigator de Surville had, that the
Tahiti Samuel Wallis had described was the same island Edward
Davis had reportedly seen in 1686, after de Surville's ship reached
Callao, Peru, in April 1770, Amat despatched two frigates commanded by Felipe González y Haedo to survey its shores and
harbours. If the island was uninhabited González was to set up 'some
sort of cairn or other monument . . . to stand as a record in the

future of the solemn possession . . . in the name of the King our Lord'. If it was inhabited he was to bring its people within Spain's orbit. If he found colonies of other European nations there, he was either to persuade the settlers to leave or, if his forces were superior, to expel them. Failing to find the island, González reconnoitred Easter Island, renaming it 'San Carlos' and claiming it for Spain, then proceeded to the coast of Chile in pursuit of further orders to search the southern American fjords and islands for any signs of a British settlement.

In October and December 1771, the Spanish Court instructed Amat to obtain possession of Tahiti, whose discovery and location were now known. In September 1772 the viceroy sent off two more ships, under the command of Dionisio de Boenechea and with two friars aboard, to claim the island and establish a mission to teach the people the virtues of friendship with Spain. Boenechea brought several Tahitians back to Peru with him. The Spanish made two more voyages to Tahiti, in 1774–75 and 1775–76, before the mission ended in failure.

Spain also explored in the northern Pacific during these years. Concerned first by reports that the Russians were about to establish posts on the northwest American coast, by other reports of British searches across North America for a navigable passage to the Pacific, and by Mulgrave's 1773 voyage towards the North Pole, the Spanish Court had the Viceroys of Mexico undertake a number of initiatives in the north. After San Blas, on the west coast of Mexico, was selected as a naval base, a settlement was established at Monterey on the coast of California in 1769. In 1774, with instructions to make friendly contact with the Indians, Juan Pérez explored the coast northwards as far as 55°N latitude, stopping at Nootka Sound on his way south again. The next year saw a second expedition under the command of Bruno de Hezeta, with Francisco Mourelle and Juan de la Bodega y Quadra among the officers. Hezeta discovered the Columbia River, while the latter pair, in the *Sonora*, reached as far as 58°30'N latitude (southern Alaska). In 1776, with information about the purpose of Cook's third voyage, Juan de Gálvez, Minister for the Indies, instructed Antonio María de Bucareli y Ursua, the Viceroy of Mexico, not to help the British explorer but instead to warn him off. In 1777, Gálvez followed up this order with instructions for a third voyage to strengthen Spain's claim to the northwest American coast. After a two-year delay, Ignacio de Arteaga sailed with two frigates. In 61°N latitude, near Prince William Sound, he claimed possession of the coast, erecting a cross to mark his visit.

Then, for a time, war prevented any further exploration in the Pacific, or any attempts to exploit the commercial prospects indicated by Cook's discoveries. In 1778, France supported Britain's rebellious American colonies, and in 1779 Spain joined it. In 1780, the northern European countries formed a League of Armed Neutrality to oppose Britain's policy of seizing their vessels which were carrying munitions to its enemies, and at the end of the year Britain declared war on Holland. The conflict was thus played out not only in European seas and in North America but in the West Indies, on the west coast of Africa, and in and around India. As soon as war ended in 1783, however, European interest in the Pacific and the countries around its rim revived, and now this interest extended beyond the government sphere to the private one.

In the first half of 1785, the French mounted what became known as Lapérouse's voyage. The origins of this expedition are curious, and show again how closely intertwined geopolitical rivalry, commercial ambition and scientific exploration were in this period. The first suggestion for it evidently came from William Bolts, a German who had served the English East India Company, then undertaken voyages to the East for Austria, during which he established a number of factories (trading posts). While at Mauritius in 1780, Bolts seems to have obtained details of Cook's third voyage, particularly noting the demand for Nootka Sound sea-otter pelts at Kamchatka and Canton. In 1784, Bolts suggested that Fleurieu, the French Minister of Marine, send two ships to develop this trade, and to expand it by exchanging the pelts for Asian goods which might then be brought back to Europe. Fleurieu explicitly linked Lapérouse's voyage to maritime and commercial considerations when he commented that the explorer 'considered it important to make it ahead of the English to the northwest coast of America'.

However, by the time it sailed, Lapérouse's expedition had been upgraded to a full scientific voyage of discovery, better equipped than any of Cook's had been. Lapérouse sailed with a retinue of scientists charged with making new observations in the fields of geography, geometry, astronomy, mechanics, physics, chemistry, anatomy, zoology, mineralogy, botany, medicine and ethnology. In his public instructions, Lapérouse was told to observe and report on the defences and trade of the European colonies he visited, on the commercial potential of the Pacific lands' products, and on the purpose of any settlement the British might have formed in the southern half of this ocean.

Jean-François de Galaup, Comte de Lapérouse, sailed from Brest with two frigates, the *Boussole* and *Astrolabe*, on 1 August 1785. Stopping at Madeira and Tenerife, on 6 November he reached the island of St Catherine off the southern coast of Brazil. After seaching the south Atlantic in vain for Isle Grande, he rounded Cape Horn and entered the Pacific in February 1786. He reached Easter Island in April, then went up to the Hawaiian Islands and on to the northwest American coast, which he reached on 23 June, in 60°N latitude. In difficult conditions of fog and rain, he worked his way down the coast, surveying and examining openings for the elusive Northwest Passage. After refreshing at Monterey he crossed the Pacific westwards, reaching Macau at the beginning of January 1787. In February he sailed to Cavite, near Manila, then headed up to the northern coasts of Asia.

Lapérouse passed between Korea and Japan at the end of May, and continued to skirt the coast north, visiting Sakhalin Island and Petropavlosk in Kamchatka, on the Bering Sea. There, he received despatches sent overland from France telling him (among other things) that the British were planting a colony at Botany Bay on the coast of New South Wales and instructing him to investigate. On 30 September he sailed south and by December reached the Samoan Islands, where he lost twelve men in a skirmish with the natives. He wrote bitterly after this untoward event:

the slightest setback would have forced me to burn one of the two frigates to man the other one and I would have had to abandon my campaign . . . if all that was needed to ease my anger was the massacre of a few Indians I had the opportunity to destroy, send to the bottom of the sea and break up a hundred canoes in which there were more than five hundred people, but I was afraid to attack the wrong victims and the call of my conscience saved their lives.

Lapérouse arrived at Botany Bay on 26 January 1788, as Governor Arthur Phillip was taking the First Fleet ships up to Port Jackson to found the convict colony at Sydney Cove. He stayed at Botany Bay six weeks, then sailed off, never to be seen again. His ships were wrecked, evidently in a cyclone, on the reef at Vanikoro, one of the Santa Cruz Islands.

In 1788, the Spanish Court accepted the Italian Alejandro Malaspina's proposal for a voyage of scientific discovery to outshine those of Cook. It was hoped that this expedition would bring 'new discoveries, careful cartographic surveys, important geodesic experiments in gravity and magnetism, botanical collections, and descriptions of each region's geography, mineral resources, commercial possibilities, political status, native peoples, and customs'. But behind these scientific purposes lurked the usual political ones, for its planners were well aware of how much the voyage might do 'to explore, examine, and knit together Madrid's far-flung empire, report on problems and possible reforms, and counter the efforts of rivals to obtain colonial possessions at Spain's expense'.

Malaspina sailed with two frigates, the *Descubierta* and the *Atrevida*, from Cádiz at the end of July 1789. After stopping at Montevideo, the Falklands and Juan Fernández Island, he spent 1790 sailing up the west coast of South America, while the scientists made observations and collected specimens. Having coasted Chile, Peru, Ecuador and Panama, he continued in 1791 past Costa Rica, Nicaragua and Guatemala to reach Acapulco, Mexico, on 27 March. On 1 May, Malaspina sailed for the northwest American coast, which he reached at the end of June, at Mulgrave Sound in 59°N latitude. After a probe northwards, he went down the coast, all the time

Eighteenth Century Voyages of Pacific Exploration, III: Lapérouse 1785–8

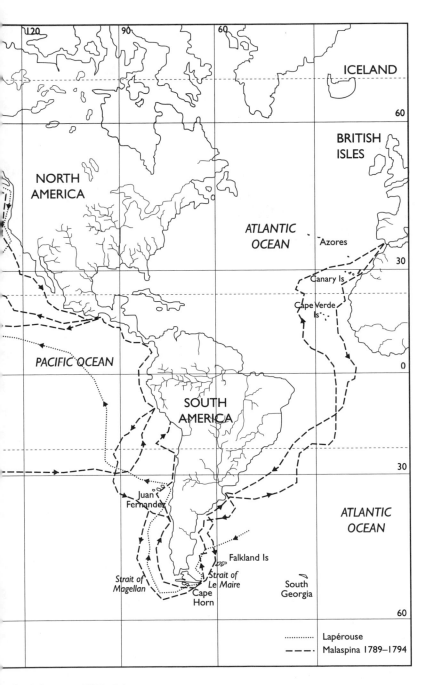

nd Malaspina 1789–94.

Fernando Brambila, Vista de la Colonia Ynglesa de Sydney en la Nueva Gales
Meridional (View of the English colony at Sydney in New South Wales)
*The officers of the Malaspina expedition were surprised by the civil order of the
New South Wales colony, and the extent of its agriculture. One wrote: 'Hardly
having been in existence for five years, it had the appearance of an old
settlement. What agreeable changes agriculture causes!'*

looking for the entrance of the Northwest Passage, and arrived back
in Acapulco on 19 October.

Leaving small parties to continue the exploration of the northwest coast, Malaspina crossed the Pacific, reaching the Marianas in
mid-February 1792 and the Philippines at the beginning of March.
For most of this year, he was occupied with a survey of the Philippine
Islands. When it was complete he sailed south, visiting New Ireland,
the Solomons, the New Hebrides, New Caledonia and New Zealand,
to reach Sydney on 11 March 1793. There he stayed four weeks,
refreshing his crews and inspecting the settlement. Passing through
the Tongan archipelago, he reached Callao again at the end of July.
After further visits to the Falklands and Montevideo, the expedition
arrived back at Cádiz in Spain on 21 September 1794.

From certain points of view, Malaspina's expedition was the
most lavish of all Enlightenment voyages of Pacific discovery, but its
full results are still not available. On his return to Spain, Malaspina

became enmeshed in political intrigue and was imprisoned; and the publication of the expedition's results languished in the Napoleonic wars. In recent years, Spanish scholars have done much new work on the expedition, with editions of journals, and catalogues of the works produced by its artists and the specimens and artifacts collected by its scientists. However, there is still no satisfactory account of the voyage in English, and only partial analyses of its results.

The lure of riches

By the mid-1780s, there was also a good deal of private interest in commercial prospects in the Pacific. Through the official account of Cook's third voyage, published in 1784, Europeans learned of the multitude of whales in the southern oceans as well as the furs available at Nootka Sound; and the British government saw both activities as being in the national interest. On the one hand, if sea-otter pelts could be obtained cheaply on the northwest coast of America and sold at a large profit in China, the pressure on the East India Company to find silver, which the Chinese demanded as payment for their silks, teas and porcelains, might be lessened. On the other hand, Britain's 'Southern' whalers (so called because they hunted south in the Atlantic rather than north towards the Arctic Circle) were eager to extend their range of operations; and the American whalers, who had remained loyal to Britain in the Revolutionary War, had lost their New England bases, so that an important industry was in limbo.

In 1785 the British government also persuaded the East India Company and the South Sea Company, which held monopolies on British trade in the East and on the west coasts of the Americas, to allow a group of merchants headed by Richard Etches and encouraged by Joseph Banks to make an experimental voyage to Nootka Sound, with the intention of developing a fur trade with Japan, Korea and China. Forming themselves into the King George's Sound Company, Etches and his partners fitted out two ships captained by Nathaniel Portlock and George Dixon, *King George* and *Queen Charlotte*, which sailed at the end of August 1785. Proceeding by way of the Falkland Islands and Cape Horn, these ships reached the northwest American coast in July 1786 and, after wintering at the Hawaiian Islands, returned there in 1787. In 1786, the company sent out two more vessels, under the command of James Colnett, which traded on the American coast in the summers of 1787 and 1788.

This officially sanctioned venture had some severe competition. Sailing from Canton, James Hanna mounted two voyages in 1785 and 1786. At the end of 1785 James Strange took two ships out from Bombay and reached the northwest coast in June 1786. Simultaneously, John Meares and William Tipping took two ships out of Calcutta. Progressively, other traders appeared—William Bolts and his former colleagues on the *Imperial Eagle*, which arrived in 1787; and New England merchants, who in September 1787 sent out two vessels under the command of John Kendrick which reached the coast twelve months later. Meares reappeared, now sailing out of Macau under the Portuguese flag; and there were also Spanish traders from the Philippines and Russian ones from Kamchatka.

Also in 1785–86 the British government persuaded the chartered trading companies to license the Southern whalers to hunt east of the Cape of Good Hope and west of Cape Horn within certain limits. These whalers quickly expanded their operations:

Year	No. of ships	Value of return cargoes
1785	11	£14 605
1786`	34	£55 753
1787	44	£107 321
1788	45	£94 957
1789	42	£97 584

The first of these whaling ships entered the Pacific towards the end of 1788, and others soon followed.

Establishing a colony

In 1786 too, laying a claim to half of New Holland and the islands 'adjacent' in the Pacific Ocean, the British government decided to establish a colony in New South Wales. Carrying some 750 convicts, 240 marines and their wives and children, and a handful of civil officials, the First Fleet under the command of Governor Arthur Phillip sailed from Portsmouth on 13 May 1787, and after stops at Rio de Janeiro and the Cape of Good Hope reached Botany Bay on 18 and 20 January 1788. Quickly deciding that Sydney Cove in Port Jackson was a more suitable site for settlement, Phillip took his people there on 26 January 1788 and set about his task.

For decades, Australian historians have usually represented this decision as the act of an incompetent government desperate to rid Britain of its criminals. But they have seen it from the perspective of twentieth-century Australia, looking backwards to the nation's convict beginnings, rather than from that of late eighteenth-century Britain, with the strategic and commercial needs of a global maritime empire in mind. Whatever the relative merits of the claims and counter-claims about the nature of the historical evidence needed for the demonstration of motives other than the dumping-of-convicts one, the plain fact is that the establishing of a colony on the east coast of New South Wales dramatically increased Britain's advantage over its rivals in the Pacific.

In the first place, the settlement at Sydney gave Britain a base adjacent to, and therefore effective control of, the *eastern* route to the Pacific, whose wind and current systems (as Cook first had found in 1772) made it faster and more reliable than the route below South America. (William Bligh was painfully to confirm this in 1788–89, when, after struggling for three weeks to round Cape Horn, he gave up in the face of contrary winds and mountainous seas, and instead sailed east for the Pacific.)

Second, the ability to provide tired and/or scurvy-stricken crews with fresh food and water was an immense boon to maritime trade and enterprise. True, the New South Wales colonists did struggle in the first years, but by the time Phillip left the colony at the end of

1792 there was no longer any doubt that it would succeed. Indeed, even before this point it had begun to offer hospitality to visiting ships' crews. Writing home in November 1791 of the good prospects to the east of New South Wales, the captain of one of the whaling vessels that constituted the Third Fleet observed: 'If a Voyage can be got upon this coast, it will make it shorter than going to Peru, and the Governor has been very attentive in sending Greens for refreshment to our Crew at different times.'

A more forceful example of how the colony might benefit ships making long voyages came ten years later. Having stayed at sea so long that his crew's bodily stores of vitamin C were entirely depleted, the French explorer Nicolas Baudin reached Sydney in mid-June 1802 with four of his crew dead, another 31 gravely ill, and everyone afflicted to some degree. One of the men described how 'their joints were stiff, their flexor [muscles were] shrunk, bowing their limbs. But their faces were the worst: leaden complexions, gums so swollen at to protrude from their mouths, ulcerated or without feeling, fetid breath.'

So weakened were these men that Governor King had to send out a party to help them bring the ship through the heads. Yet the health of most was restored after a few days on Sydney's fruits and vegetables:

> *nearly all our scorbutic patients were so ill, that it would have required several days to convey half of them on shore: two of them died the day after we anchored, but all the rest recovered so rapidly, as to strike us with astonishment; not one of those who had been landed died, and in a few days, those who were actually on the brink of the grave, recovered their health. We were, in short, lost in wonder at the magical effect of the country and the vegetables upon a disorder, to counteract which, all the medicines on board ship, all the most active operations, and energetic attentions, had proved fruitless.*

Third, the possession of a harbour as good as Port Jackson offered Britain a great advantage. Phillip, who had seen many, described it as 'the finest harbour in the world, in which a thousand sail of the line may ride in the most perfect security'. This was a judgment that officers of rival marines shared. Malaspina, for example, remarked that 'It is impossible to describe adequately the beauty of the harbour and the admiration it should arouse in any seafarer who enters it.' In 1792, Henry Dundas, then Home Secretary, wrote to Phillip of 'the advantages which must always be derived from a port so capacious and secure as Port Jackson'.

Fourth, if this settlement could offer naval materials as well, so much the better, for without masts and spars, canvas, cordage and cables eighteenth-century ships could not be sailed. Normal problems of maintenance and replacement increased the farther a ship went from a well-equipped dockyard; and at this period Europeans supplied even their dockyards in India largely from home. Despite some historians' doubts, there is good evidence that the British were interested in Norfolk Island's and New Zealand's pines and flax; and that the proximity of these materials was one of the motives for the New South Wales colonisation. 'Besides the removal of a dreadful Banditti from this Country', Evan Nepean, the Undersecretary at the Home Department, wrote in October 1786,

many Advantages are likely to be derived from this intended Settlement. Some of the Timber is reported to be fit for Naval purposes particularly Masts, which the Fleet employed occasionally in the East Indies frequently stand[s] in need of, and which it cannot be supplied with but from Europe. But above all, the Cultivation of the Flax Plant seems to be the most considerable object. This Plant has been found in that Neighbourhood in the most luxuriant State, and small quantities have been brought to Europe and manufactured, and, from its superior quality, it will it is hoped soon become an Article of Commerce from that Country.

Finally, a base at Sydney could serve as the hub of a network of

❧ SCURVY, SCOURGE OF SAILORS ❧

When Lord Anson left England in 1740, he had eight ships and 1955 sailors. When he returned four years later, he had one ship and only 145 of his original men. Almost 1300 had died of illness, approximately 1000 from scurvy.

Scurvy, the disease caused by lack of vitamin C, was the scourge of sailors on long voyages until the end of the eighteenth century. Without fresh food, the body's store of vitamin C lasts for only about 70 to 90 days. After that, the skin and tongue break out in ulcers, the gums swell, bleed and go black, the teeth become loose and the breath foul. The muscles shrink, the skin bruises easily, the person becomes weak and fatigued, and death quickly follows.

Although he did not know about vitamins or realise that scurvy was a deficiency disease, the British naval surgeon James Lind reported in 1753 that orange and lemon juices were specific cures. As well as urging that sea voyagers eat fresh foods at every opportunity, Lind recommended that ships be kept clean and hammocks dry, seamen be made to change into dry clothes when they came off watch, and alcohol consumption be reduced. Lind's advice was sound. We now know that citrus juices contain high levels of vitamin C and that salt intake, labour in wet and cold conditions and alcohol all cause the body to use up its stores of this vitamin faster than usual.

Cook took a number of supposed antiscorbutics (anti-scurvy foods) with him on his three voyages, including malt concentrate, sauerkraut and essence of lemon. But because he gave all of them to men showing symptoms of scurvy, he failed to arrive at Lind's insight that

sea routes linking New South Wales to the East Indies, India, China and North and South America by easy stages between islands that Britain had also claimed possession of. This potential network had been described in detail in 1783 by James Matra, on whose proposal the British government had based its decision to colonise; and it was well understood by Britain's rivals. In 1788 the experienced Spanish naval officer Francisco Muñoz y San Clemente reported to Madrid that the British settlements in the southwest Pacific 'will have a Navy of their own, obtaining from the southern region everything necessary to create it, and when they have it ready it was lemon juice that cured the condition. Malt contains no vitamin C and sauerkraut has only a little, yet when he returned to England Cook sang the praises of both. In doing so, he handicapped the Royal Navy's scurvy prevention efforts for another 25 years. It was not until the end of the eighteenth century, when Sir Gilbert Blane, one of Lind's followers, persuaded the Admiralty to issue lemon juice to all sailors, and Lord Nelson kept his crews healthy by obtaining large quantities of citrus fruits from the Mediterranean islands, that the problem was solved.

(Joseph Banks, it seems, was more up-to-date on the treatment of scurvy than Cook. He wrote in his journal for 1 April 1769:

As my complaint has something in it that at least puts me in mind of the scurvy I took up the lemon Juice put up by Dr Hulmes directions.)

Still, until the *Endeavour's* crew were laid low with dysentery and malaria at Batavia, the health record on the ship was good, with scurvy appearing at only irregular intervals. This was because Cook had followed Lind's general regimen rigorously and fed his crew fresh foods at every opportunity. As Cook became more familiar with the Pacific Ocean, he tended to refresh his crews at intervals of roughly 50 to 70 days. As scurvy is quickly cured by even small intakes of vitamin C, this meant he had little trouble with the disease on the second and third voyages. On the second, for example, he lost only four men on the *Resolution*, and none from scurvy. Unwittingly, he had acted to keep the scourge at bay.

formed they will be able to invade our neighbouring possessions with expeditions less costly and surer than from the ports of England, and it will not be difficult to foretell, even now, which will be their first conquests'. The navigator Alejandro Malaspina thought that one of Britain's aims was to see 'that Holland and Spain bear the principal costs of the outbreak of war, with the aid of the Islands of the Pacific for the necessary maintenance of squadrons, or corsairs, which would indiscriminately direct their course now towards Asia, now towards America'. And he thought that no other settlement could be 'more terrible for Spain than Port Jackson'. From it, 'with the greatest ease

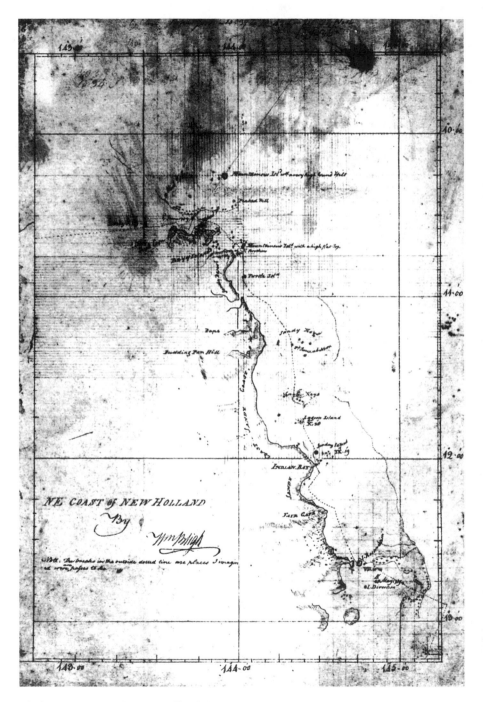

Bligh, NE Coast of New Holland (1789).

a crossing of two or three months through healthy Climates, and a secure navigation, could bring to our defenceless Coasts two or three thousand castaway bandits to serve interpolated with an excellent body of regular Troops'.

The colonisation of New South Wales also led immediately to some incidental Pacific discoveries, as captains of the First Fleet ships took various routes home. Making a great sweep east, north and then west to reach Canton, Thomas Gilbert in the *Charlotte* and John Marshall in the *Scarborough* found the island groups named after them. And in 1789, during the course of his epic voyage of 5400 km in an open boat from the vicinity of Tonga to Timor after he had been thrown off the *Bounty*, William Bligh obtained details of the small islands to the south of New Guinea.

As a result of all these voyages, official, semi-official and private, by 1790 Europeans had accumulated a good deal of additional information about wind and current systems, sailing conditions, and harbours and places of refreshment in the north and south Pacific Ocean.

7
A EUROPEAN PACIFIC

British plans for commercial empire, 1785–1804

In the 1770s and 1780s, Spain and France were
following the agenda in oceanic exploration set
earlier by Britain; Britain was adding a new ele-
ment to that agenda by colonising New South
Wales; and independent traders were beginning
to develop the Pacific's commercial possibilities.

The next phase of the European exploration
of the Pacific Ocean arose from Britain's seeking
massively to expand this commerce. In the
autumn of 1786 and the spring and summer of
1787, key members of the government developed
a grandiose scheme for a triangular exchange of
European, American and Asian goods. The plan
was to trade British manufactures for South
American silver and North American furs; then
silver and furs for Chinese and other Asian
goods; and then to take part of the Asian goods
back to the Spanish colonies in America, and part to Europe.

Before they could implement this scheme, the British first had to:

- develop and control reliable sailing routes to and from the Pacific;
- gain formal access to markets (since both Spain and China
  insisted on rigidly controlling commerce with other nations);
- find merchants willing to conduct trade;
- free these merchants from the obstructions created by the East
  India Company's and South Sea Company's monopolies.

At this time there were—in very broad terms—only four possible
sea routes from Europe to the Pacific: the western one around South

America; the eastern one past southern Australia or New Zealand; the route through the East Indies up to the Philippines and China; and—if it existed—the one through the Northwest Passage. In the 1760s, as we have seen, Britain had tried to secure the western route by colonising the Falklands, but Spain's opposition had forced it to give up this base. There is no evidence that the British government hoped to recolonise the Falklands, but in 1789 it did prepare an expedition to survey the southwest coast of Africa and various islands in the south Atlantic. The New South Wales settlement gave it access to the eastern route. At the end of the 1780s, with advice from Lord Mulgrave, the Admiralty surveyed islands in the Indian Ocean and established a base on one of the Andamans, and the East India Company settled the island of Penang, at the entrance to the Straits of Malacca.

In 1787 the government sent Colonel Charles Cathcart to negotiate with the Chinese for access to their markets, and for the right to use an island or harbour to the north of Canton as an emporium. Henry Dundas, the leading member of the India Board, told Cathcart to assure the Chinese that Britain's views were 'purely commercial[,] having not even a Wish for territory'; and that 'should a new Establishment be conceded', he was to 'endeavour to obtain free permission of ingress and regress for Ships of all Nations, upon paying certain settled Duties, if so required by the Chinese Government'. Cathcart never reached his destination, dying off the coast of Indochina in 1788.

The fur traders and Southern whalers were to be the vectors of trade. They would carry manufactures outwards, exchange them for other goods wherever they had the opportunity, and in this way criss-cross the ocean like bees gathering nectar.

The British government also negotiated with the chartered companies for permission for these merchants to operate within the areas of company monopolies. As the South Sea Company had been moribund for decades, it was easy to obtain the agreement of its directors. The East India Company, however, guarded its privileges jealously. The government did gradually secure concessions, but some officials hoped to remove the company's monopoly when its charter came up for renewal in 1793.

The Nootka Sound Crisis of 1790 gave Britain the opportunity to complete the arrangements it needed to promote trade. In 1788, Spain had decided to re-assert its claims to a monopoly of navigation and trade in the Pacific and to possession of the northwest American coast. Accordingly, the Viceroy of Mexico sent Estéban José Martínez in two vessels to search the coast as far north as Alaska for other European nationals, and to take possession of sites suitable for settlement. Martínez found that the Russians had made trading camps at a number of places, and that the governor of Kamchatka intended to establish a fortified one at Nootka Sound. He also learned of the activities of British and American fur traders. On his return to San Blas, he urged the viceroy to establish a Spanish base at Nootka Sound and resist these encroachments. Accepting this suggestion, the viceroy sent Martínez north again in the spring of 1789.

By this time, the Meares and Etches groups had decided to join forces so as to develop the fur trade in a more orderly way, a move which gave the overall command of their five vessels to James Colnett. When he sailed from Canton to renew the trade in April 1789, Colnett had orders to consolidate Meares's settlement at Nootka Sound. The proposed factory was to be 'a solid establishment, and not one that is to be abandon'd at pleasure'. To this end, Colnett took with him 29 Chinese workmen and building materials, and the framework of a small ship. Arriving at Nootka Sound on 2 July, he found that Martínez had already seized two of his group's vessels, while leaving American ones untouched. When Colnett protested, Martínez seized Colnett's *Argonaut* as well. He then seized a fourth ship and sent it and the *Argonaut*, with their crews imprisoned, to San Blas, where a number of British seamen died. As he waited to be resupplied, Martínez used the Chinese labourers Colnett had brought to begin establishing a base himself.

These actions in the northern Pacific were paralleled by others on the coast of Patagonia. In April 1789 at Port Desire, a Spanish commodore ordered away the *Sappho* and *Elizabeth and Margaret*, two whaling ships that had called in to get wood and water. The British captains said they were not aware that Spanish sovereignty extended over this 'desert' coast. The Spaniard replied that it extended not only over the coast but over the nearby ocean, and that he had orders to keep foreign ships out of both. The stage was set for international conflict.

For much of 1790, Britain and Spain argued over rights to navigate in the southern Atlantic and the Pacific, and to possess territory bordering them. Spain had long insisted it had an exclusive claim to these areas based on the papal bulls of 1493 and the Treaty of Tordesillas of 1494. Now it added that its voyages during the 1770s had also given it a claim based on first discovery. Britain replied that it could 'never in any shape accede to those Claims of Exclusive Sovereignty, Commerce and Navigation' made by Spain. British subjects, the government said, had 'an unquestionable Right to a free and undisturbed Enjoyment of the Benefits of Commerce, Navigation and Fishery, and also to the Possession of such Establishments, as they may form, with the Consent of the Natives, in Places not occupied by other European nations'.

From February until the end of April, the British planned to send warships via New South Wales to rendezvous with others from India at either Tahiti or Hawaii, then sail on to Nootka Sound to expel the Spanish and set up a base. But when John Meares reached London, claiming that he had already purchased land from the Nootka and started a settlement when Martínez arrived, the government decided to confront the issue head-on in Europe. It mobilised the fleet and gave Spain an ultimatum. Unable to obtain France's help, Spain was forced to capitulate to Britain's overwhelming naval superiority, and in October it formally conceded Britain's right to settle the Nootka Sound region on the basis of prior discovery, negotiation with the indigenous people, and effective occupation. Each country agreed not to 'disturb or molest' the other's people 'either in navigating or carrying on their fisheries in the Pacific Ocean or in the South Seas, or in landing on the coasts of those seas in places not already occupied, for the purpose of carrying on their commerce with the natives of the country or of making settlements there'. The days when a nation could claim territory 'by grant of a Pope' or 'by discovery without absolute settlement' were over.

Prime Minister Pitt told Parliament in the middle of the Nootka

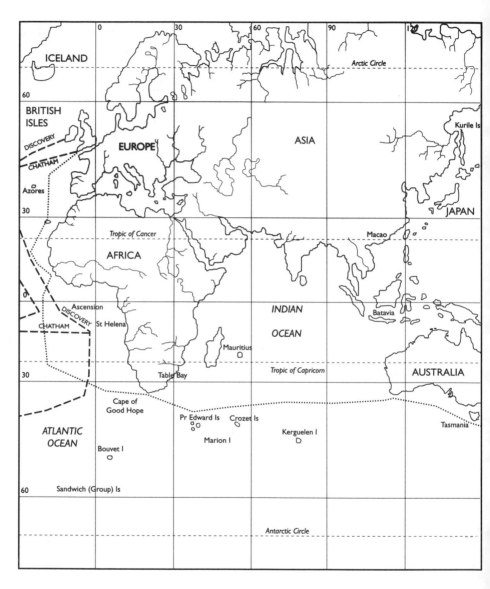

Eighteenth Century Voyages of Pacific Exploration, IV: Vancouver 1791–5.

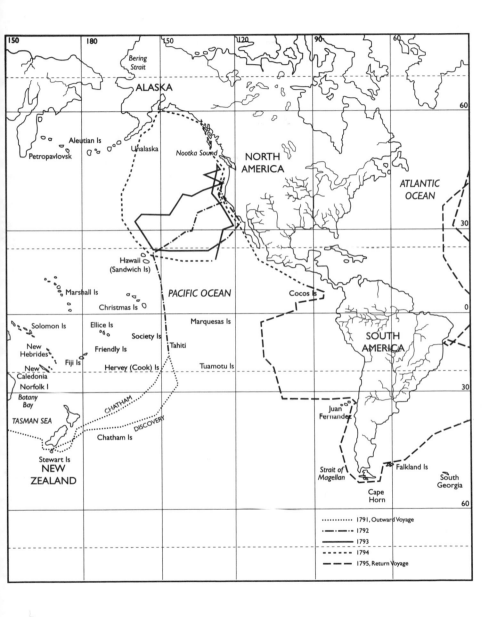

Sound crisis that, if accepted, Spain's claim to 'exclusive sovereignty, navigation and commerce' in and around the Pacific would

deprive this country of the means of extending its navigation and fishery in the southern ocean, and would go towards excluding his majesty's subjects from an infant trade, the future extension of which could not but be essentially beneficial to the commercial interests of Great Britain;

and when he announced the terms of the agreement with Spain, Henry Dundas observed that he and his colleagues had been contending, not 'for a few miles, but a large world'.

Opening the world

Just how large the British thought their imperial world could be soon became apparent. At the beginning of 1791, the government sent George Vancouver to accept the restitution of what Martínez had seized at Nootka Sound, and to survey the tortuous northwest coast of America in a final search for the Pacific entrance of the Northwest Passage. Part of the motivation for this was the need to counter the likely political and commercial effects of Malaspina's voyage, and in particular to forestall him in discovery, for if the Spanish were to find the Northwest Passage first, they would gain control of it by settling near its entrance. As well, the British were anxious to secure all of what is now western Canada,

[it being his Majesty's intention] that an Establishment should be formed . . . with a view to the opening a Commercial intercourse with the Natives, as also for establishing a line of communication across the Continent of America, and thereby to

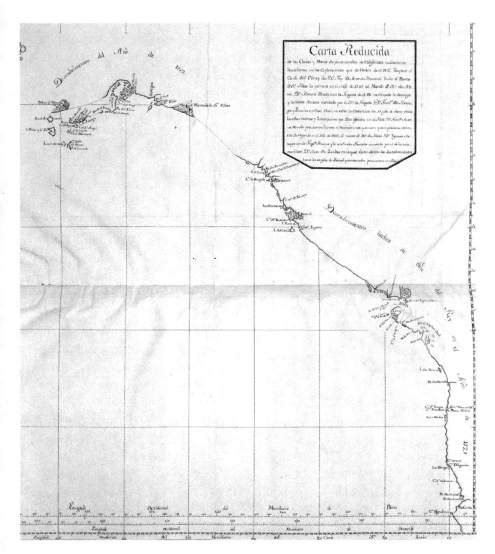

Bodega y Quadra, 'Carta Reducida de las Costas y Mares . . . de Californias'
(Reduced Chart of the Coasts and Seas . . . of California).

prevent any future intrusion, by securing to this Country the
possession of those parts which lye at the back of Canada and
Hudson's Bay, as well as the Navigation by such Lakes as are
already known or may hereafter be discovered.

Sailing in the *Discovery* and *Chatham* in April 1791, Vancouver went via the Cape of Good Hope to touch at the southwestern corner of Australia, where he found King George Sound at the end of September. He then crossed to Dusky Sound in New Zealand and went up to Tahiti, which he reached at the end of December, and on to the Hawaiian Islands. He struck the northwest coast of America at Cape Cabrillo in 39°N latitude in April 1792. For the next three summers, he traced that much-indented coastline from the Strait of Juan de Fuca to Alaska, in a meticulous yet fruitless search for the Northwest Passage. The resulting survey of some 16 000 km of coastline was a model of scientific exactitude. Vancouver also negotiated with the Spanish over Nootka Sound, only to discover complexities that were not covered in his instructions; and he demonstrated the great usefulness to European activity in the northern Pacific of the Hawaiian Islands, where he wintered. The expedition returned to Europe in September 1795.

In these same years Captain Juan Francisco de la Bodega y Quadra, sent by the Viceroy of Mexico to make the required restitution at Nootka Sound, also explored sections of the northwest coast, even as he was negotiating—charmingly yet futilely—issues of sovereignty with Vancouver.

At the height of the Nootka Sound crisis, the British government had sent Captain John Blankett to the East. His first aim was to escort the East India Company ships from Canton to the Bay of Bengal; his second was to reinforce the India squadron in any attack on Spanish settlements in the Philippines or the Americas. If war did not break out, then Blankett was to investigate the coasts and trade of northern Asia and its adjacent islands. Blankett sailed in August, and reached the Cape of Good Hope in October. From there, he took a route past Timor up through the Moluccas to Canton, not only because this was 'the clearest way' given the season, but also because 'it might lead to establish the right of the King's subjects to the free Navigation of those Seas'. He reached Canton at the end of February 1791.

As he sailed, Blankett looked and listened carefully so he could report to his government in detail on strategy and trade. He found that the Dutch empire was in decline, and thought that if Cape

Town were declared a free port, then 'America and Africa might be furnished from thence with all the produce of India & China, & many parts of Europe and Asia would find a vent & return for many of their productions, without being subject to the risque & expense of a longer Navigation'. He also believed that 'our Exports to China might be greatly extended'. From one of the Nootka Sound fur traders, he learned of additional discoveries on the northwest American coast and in the Seas of Japan, where he thought (as he had twenty years earlier) that 'much may be done by way of Commerce'. From the captain of the *Panther* he learned details of the Pelew Islands, which might give warships 'command [of] the Passage from North America to Asia more particularly that of the Philippines'. From what he could learn, the Spanish seemed to have let Manila's defences fall into disrepair and 'had no Sea force' there. Blankett's information contributed to the government's preparations for a second diplomatic mission to China under Lord Macartney in 1792–94.

In February and March 1791 the government negotiated with the East India Company to extend the range of the fur traders' and whalers' activities. After bitter argument, the company agreed to let the fur traders operate along the western coast of North America and the coasts of Asia south to Canton, and let the whalers hunt off South America and in the western Pacific east of 135°E longitude and south of 10°S latitude—that is, in the waters around New South Wales.

By 1793, then, Britain had established its right to navigate and trade in and around the Pacific Ocean, and made it easier for fur traders and whalers to do so; the Penang and Sydney settlements were developing satisfactorily; Vancouver was continuing the search for the Northwest Passage; Macartney was making another attempt to obtain more liberal access to China (and northern Asia in general). The only prerequisite for large-scale trade with and across the Pacific not yet in place was a base on the western route to this ocean. The Admiralty soon took this up, engaging James Colnett to 'perform the service of searching for Places in the Pacific Oceans, and also in the South Atlantic for South whale Fisheries that voyaged round Cape Horn to refresh at'. When war broke out with France, Colnett sailed in a private ship, the *Rattler*, but still followed Admiralty instructions. In 1794, he inspected numerous islands off the west coast of South America with an eye not only for harbours and indigenous resources, but also for strategic and commercial prospects. He thought Plata Island, for example, would be 'an excellent Station in any future war with Spain, both as a look out, and for landing the sick'. But he reserved his highest praise for the Galapagos Islands. They were, he said, 'a half way house to all vessels, bound round Cape Horn to any part No. of the equator, or a place for whalers to refit, fishing either in the No. or S. Pacific[,] Gulf of Panama, or among those Isles or as a rendezvous in another war with Spain for his British Majesty's Ships'. 'I think it one of the most desirable Spots under heaven to our Country', he continued, '& the best opportunity to take advantage and the India Company to settle it, it would in a short time return them innumerable riches'.

National rivalries

As the Vancouver expedition sailed, so too did another French one. In 1791 the National Assembly authorised a voyage to search for the missing Lapérouse and examine as yet unknown parts of Australia. Joseph-Antoine Bruni d'Entrecasteaux sailed with two ships, *Recherche* and *Espérance*, from Brest at the end of September 1791, with a scientific party that included astronomers, zoologists, botanists, geographers, draughtsmen, a mineralogist and a gardener. He reached the Cape of Good Hope in January 1792, then crossed the southern Indian Ocean to d'Entrecasteaux Channel in Tasmania. From here, he sailed north to look for signs of Lapérouse's expedition in New Caledonia, New Ireland and the Admiralty Archipelago, before passing north and west of New Guinea to Amboina, where he refreshed in September and October 1792. He then coasted western and southern Australia, arriving back at Tasmania in January 1793. He went through the Kermadec to the Tongan Islands, then back past New Caledonia, but found no sign of Lapérouse. Both Entrecasteaux and his second-in-command died in July 1793, and with the crews sick and exhausted and the ships decrepit, the junior officers decided to proceed to the Dutch ports in the East Indies. There, the tensions of war and the French Revolution saw the expedition fall apart. Its charts and natural history collections fell into British hands, and its survivors returned gradually in small groups to Europe.

The British also made some incidental discoveries in the western Pacific in the 1790s. Sent to capture the *Bounty* mutineers, Captain Edward Edwards was forced into a similar position to Bligh's when the *Pandora* was wrecked on the Great Barrier Reef and he took the survivors in open boats to Batavia. With the *Providence* and *Assistant*, Bligh again went south of New Guinea in 1793 on his second, successful, voyage to transport breadfruit trees from Tahiti to Jamaica. These voyages provided additional details of islands in the Coral Sea and of the best way through Torres Strait. From Sydney, too, the British made probes up and down the coast of New South Wales, which culminated in the discovery by George Bass and Matthew Flinders of Bass Strait and their circumnavigation of Tasmania in 1797–98. And private traders began collecting cargoes of masts and spars in New Zealand.

The circumnavigation of Australia and the detailed charting of its coasts were the last major tasks of the phase of Pacific exploration that began in 1749. At the turn of the new century, France and Britain each mounted expeditions. Nicolas Baudin sailed with two ships, the *Géographe* and *Naturaliste*, from France in October 1800, accompanied by 22 scientists, artists, draftsmen and gardeners. The expedition sighted the southwest corner of Australia in mid-May 1801, and for the next two years Baudin and his junior captain, Jacques-Félix-Emmanuel Hamelin, accurately charted the western and southern coasts of the mainland and the coasts of Tasmania, while the scientists gathered zoological, botanical and mineral specimens and ethnographic information, particularly about the Tasmanian Aborigines. The expedition returned with about 18 500 zoological specimens, including some 2500 that were new, and Antoine Laurent de Jussieu, professor of botany at the Musée d'Histoire Naturelle, considered the botanical collection the finest ever to reach France.

Partly in competition, in these same years the British

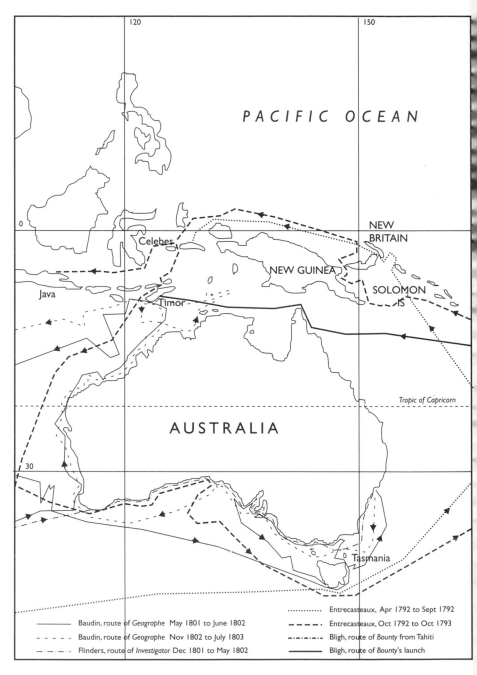

120

150

PACIFIC OCEAN

NEW
BRITAIN

Celebes

NEW GUINEA

SOLOMON
IS

Java

Timor

0

Tropic of Capricorn

AUSTRALIA

30

Tasmania

————— Baudin, route of *Geographe* May 1801 to June 1802

- - - - Baudin, route of *Geographe* Nov 1802 to July 1803

-·-·-·- Flinders, route of *Investigator* Dec 1801 to May 1802

············· Entrecasteaux, Apr 1792 to Sept 1792

- - - - Entrecasteaux, Oct 1792 to Oct 1793

-··-··-··- Bligh, route of *Bounty* from Tahiti

————— Bligh, route of *Bounty*'s launch

Eighteenth Century Voyages of Pacific Exploration, V: Bligh 1789

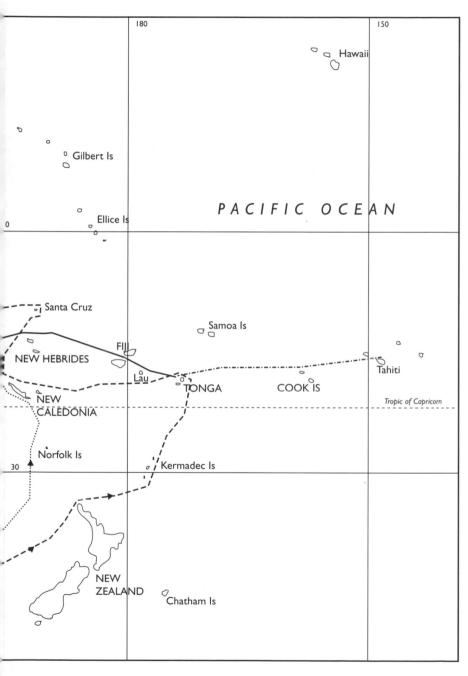

ntrecasteaux 1791–3, Baudin 1801–3 and Flinders 1802–3.

Freycinet, Carte Générale de la Nouvelle Hollande.

government sent Matthew Flinders in the *Investigator* to survey the Australian coasts, which he also did very precisely. Like Baudin, Flinders was accompanied by a party of scientists, and his expedition sent extensive collections home. The botanist Robert Brown, for example, gathered some 3400 specimens, of which about 2000 were new.

Imperial rivalry remained a key motive for exploration. Baudin gave the name *Terre Napoléon* to those parts of Australia not claimed by the British, and while at Sydney, some of his men talked loosely of plans to establish a settlement at Storm Bay (Hobart). On learning of this, Governor King sent an officer to examine Port Phillip, King Island, and other sites for 'the best situation for settlements, in which you will have a view to the commercial advantages, access for vessels, obtaining fresh water, and its defence'. He gave this officer a letter to Baudin requesting an explanation of the rumours, and he wrote home to the government describing his measures to confirm 'His Majesty's Right to [Van Diemen's Land] being within the limits of this Territory'. Baudin's reply from King Island was not encouraging. The British party had arrived too late to prevent the French establishing their right to possess it, he wrote; and he pointed out that a Dutchman had first discovered Van Diemen's Land.

His suspicions now confirmed, in September 1803 King sent a party to settle Risdon Cove in the Derwent estuary. Simultaneously, Lord Hobart, the Secretary of State for the Colonies, acted to counter the French threat, appointing David Collins to head a settlement at Port Phillip, and equipping the *Calcutta* to carry him and some 450 marines and convicts out. Collins reached his destination in October 1803. Disappointed with the site he chose on the Mornington Peninsula, he shifted to the Derwent estuary in February 1804. Six months later, the settlers at Risdon Cove came down to join him. In October 1804, King sent another party to settle Port Dalrymple (Launceston). By the end of this year, the British had consolidated their claim to the southeastern coasts of Australia and secured Bass Strait.

By this time, Europeans had learnt enough about the Pacific's wind and current systems and its best stopping-off places to be able to navigate it easily. Indeed, they had effectively established a network of routes linking Europe to the Pacific Rim. In its broad aspects, this network meant that ships taking the eastern route outwards came through the southern Indian Ocean east around Tasmania and up to Sydney. (From 1800 onwards, through Bass Strait became the preferred path.) From Sydney, ships would sail southeastwards for South America and Europe via New Zealand; or go up to the centre of the ocean via New Zealand and Tahiti; on to the northeast quarter via the Hawaiian Islands; or up to the Philippines and China via the islands of Melanesia, Samoa or Fiji; or northwest to the East Indies and India via Torres Strait or above New Guinea. Ships following the western route would round Cape Horn, then work up the western coasts of the Americas to Hawaii or Nootka Sound, before crossing to China or coming down through the island clusters of the central Pacific to Sydney. Thickets of European masts were rising above the Pacific and acres of European sails were spreading over it; carried out by Cook on his third voyage, by Lapérouse and Bligh, and especially by the New South Wales colonists, European plants and animals were establishing themselves on its islands and shores; and the lives of its indigenous inhabitants were changed forever by contact with another world.

8
JAMES COOK IN TIME

Conclusion

As a result of the European exploration of the Pacific Ocean in the
second half of the eighteenth century, the peoples of the islands and
countries in and around it were colonised financially or politically by
the European powers. It is all too
sadly true that for many indigenous
peoples this proved disastrous, as it
did for sea creatures such as whales
and seals.

But from the points of view of improvements in navigational
techniques and the expansion of scientific, geographical and ethnographic knowledge, this exploration was an extraordinary human
achievement—all the more so when we remember that it was done
in comparatively small ships whose crews lived in very cramped
circumstances and were often debilitated by hunger and thirst. The
use of reliable chronometers let seamen calculate longitude with
accuracy, and improvements in health measures enabled them to
keep their ships at sea much longer than earlier explorers had been
able to. In less than 50 years, the supposed enormous southern
continent and the supposed Northwest Passage were removed from
the map of the world and the missing coastlines of Australia,
northwest America and northeast Asia drawn in. Islands and water-
ways lost to European view for up to 200 years—the Marquesas
Islands, the Solomons, the New Hebrides, Torres Strait—were rediscovered, and numerous others were discovered. Indeed, all the major
and many of the minor island clusters were accurately located, and
the great ocean's vastness was fully understood for the first time.
Thousands of kilometres of the continental shores that fringe it
were charted with unprecedented accuracy. Countless botanical,

Australia in Relation to the Pacific Rim.

Coat of Arms granted posthumously to Captain James Cook (1785)
It was rare for a commoner to be granted a Coat of Arms. That George III accorded one to Cook's family after his death is a sign of the esteem in which the great navigator was held by the British nation.

zoological and mineral specimens were collected, and a wealth of ethnographic detail recorded. In the duration of one European lifetime (say, that of Sir Joseph Banks, 1743–1820), explorers unveiled the features of one-third of the globe's surface, and recorded and publicised them. It is no exaggeration to say that Europeans gathered more information about the world in this half-century than in any previous one.

This was the work of many men, and of the governments, national marines and private interests which supported them; and the activities of each decade built cumulatively on those of the preceding one. Also, it went forward within the shared conceptual frameworks of the scientific Enlightenment and European commerce. But one name stands out above all the rest. On receiving Captain Clerke's letters sent overland from Kamchatka, Lord Sandwich, who had done so much to oversee the exploration of the Pacific, wrote to Joseph Banks: 'What is uppermost in our mind allways must come out first, poor captain Cooke is no more.'

By the time this news arrived, Cook's fame had spread throughout Europe and to North America. In the years that followed, the British made him a national hero and posthumously offered him a great variety of tributes—a family coat of arms, medals, memorials, speeches, even pantomimes. Nor were the accolades solely British. In 1779, when Cook's ships were expected back in European waters, Benjamin Franklin offered them the protection of the Congress of the rebellious colonies, telling American naval commanders that they should 'treat the said Captain Cook and his People with all Civility and Kindness, affording them as common Friends to Mankind all the Assistance in your Power which they may happen to stand in need of'. France also offered this protection. In 1788, Lapérouse told the British officers at Sydney that Cook had 'left nothing to those who might follow in his track to describe, or fill up'. Fifty years later, Jules-Sébastien-César Dumont d'Urville remarked that in his own extensive explorations in the Pacific, he had felt himself 'haunted' by Cook's presence.

Inevitably, some of this praise was based on conceptions of manhood and nationhood, and of racial and cultural superiority which are now outmoded and sometimes distasteful. But even when

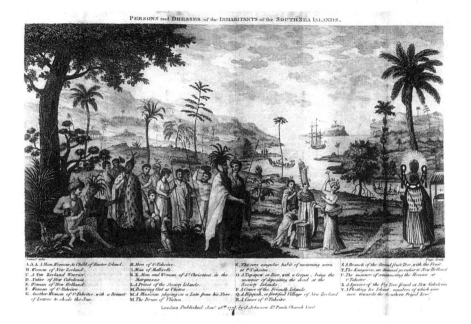

[Anon.], Persons and Dresses of the Inhabitants of the South Sea Islands
*In the second half of the eighteenth century, European curiosity about lands and
peoples elsewhere greatly increased. The voyages of Cook and the other Pacific
explorers brought knowledge of many peoples and cultures, of whose existence
Europeans had previously had no inkling.*

due allowance is made for changed attitudes, there is a singularity
to Cook himself, and a quality to his voyages, that set both apart.
Of all those who have written about James Cook, no one, it seems
to me, has better understood his historical significance than one of
his colleagues from his second voyage. In an essay published in 1787,
Georg Forster said:

*His mind, which knew no idleness, was constantly reflecting on
means of relieving the hardships of his people's harsh way of
life and in so doing to lengthen the duration of the voyage, to
expand the scope of his discoveries and to enrich our knowledge
of the realm of truth by means of new observations on nature,*

*on human as well as on animal vegetable and inanimate bodies.
In so far as it was consistent with the planned instructions of
the voyage or could serve the more complete execution of the
same, he tarried in his newly discovered countries and
organized, sometimes in person and sometimes with the help of
his companions, those careful investigations which, as long as
the art of printing immortalises thoughts, will be read with
sympathy and understanding as sources of the most useful,
dependable and agreeable instruction . . . No one knew the
value of a fleeting moment better and no one used it so
scrupulously as he. In the same period of time no one has ever
extended the bounds of our knowledge to such a degree.*

Turning to the subject of ethnographic discovery, Forster continued:

*Let us look . . . at the most important object of our researches,
at our own species; at just how many races, with whose very
name we were formerly unacquainted, have been described down
to their smallest characteristics throught the memorable efforts
of this great man! Their physical diversity, their temperament,
their customs, their mode of life and dress, their form of
government, their religion, their ideas of science and works
of art, in short everything was collected by Cook for
his contemporaries and for posterity with fidelity and
tireless diligence.*

Like Georg Forster, Cook's British contemporaries praised him greatly for his 'humanity'—that is, for his humane and generous treatment of the non-Europeans he met. Lately, some writers have derided this view, pointing to Cook's behaviour during his third voyage. It is true that Cook then lapsed from his own high ideals. But these lapses were not publicised at the time, so that what the people of his era saw was an explorer who did take a different approach to other cultures from that of his predecessors—and as many of his contemporaries would have done if they had had the means. Compare, for example, Cook's attitude to the Maori who killed Furneaux's boat crew with Lapérouse's bitter lament after the death of his men at Samoa (pp. 76–7). In proceeding as he did, Cook offered powerful insights into how Europeans might best view and respond to non-Europeans, and not inflict upon them the rapacious and murderous behaviour that had marked the European conquest of the Americas. As Cook's contemporary Hannah More put it:

> *Had those advent'rous spirits, who explore*
> *Through ocean's trackless wastes, the far sought shore,*
> *Whether of wealth insatiate, or of power,*
> *Conquerors who waste, or ruffians who devour:*
> *Had these possess'd, O Cook! thy gentle mind,*
> *Thy love of arts, thy love of humankind;*
> *Had these pursu'd thy mild and lib'ral plan,*
> *DISCOVERERS had not been a curse to man!*

Cook's actions and discoveries reinforced the growing discourse on the 'humanity' of common people, non-European as well as European. As More continued, if other discoverers had behaved as humanely as Cook:

> *Then, bless'd Philanthropy! thy social hands,*
> *Had link'd disserver'd worlds in brothers' bands;*
> *Careless, if colour, or if clime divide;*
> *Then lov'd, and loving, man had liv'd, and died.*

One powerful manifestation of this understanding in the period appeared in the anti-slavery movement. Another came in the literary movement known as Romanticism, which extolled the virtues of humble and rural life.

James Cook was an extraordinary person. As he said in explaining the plain style of his account of his second voyage, he did not have 'the advantage of much school education', but rather was 'constantly at sea from his youth', where he 'passed through all the stations belonging to a seaman, from an apprentice boy in the coal trade, to a Post Captain in the Royal Navy'. In his quest to be the first discoverer—even of nothing more than sands and shoals—he spent years ranging the Pacific Ocean, from Australia and New Zealand to the Americas, from the Antarctic to the Arctic Circle. Awarding Cook the Copley Medal, Sir John Pringle, the President of the Royal Society, pointed out how he had 'not only discovered, but surveyed, vast tracts of new coasts'; and how he had 'dispelled the illusion of a *terra australis incognita*, and fixed the bounds of the habitable earth, as well as those of the navigable ocean, in the southern hemisphere'. He was (in the words of another contemporary) 'the ablest and most renowned Navigator this or any country hath produced'; and he marked the imagination of his age as profoundly as a Newton or a Darwin.

But there is another side to Cook's life which is almost hidden to history. On 21 December 1762, he had married Elizabeth Batts in the Barking parish church. Cook's work meant that the couple were apart much more than they were together. But in the intervals between surveys and voyages, they evidently had a normal family life. They had six children—James in October 1763, Nathaniel in December 1764, Elizabeth in 1767, Joseph in August 1768, George in June 1772, Hugh in May 1776. Three of these—Elizabeth, Joseph, and George—died very young, and while their father was away. Elizabeth Cook lived to the great age of 93. During her long life she guarded her and her husband's privacy, and before she died destroyed his letters to her.

That percipient observer of people James Boswell met her in the interval between the second and third voyages, when Cook had been taken up by members of the Royal Society. He wrote of dining with the Cooks at Sir John Pringle's house on 2 April 1776:

I talked a great deal with him today, as he was very obliging and communicative. He seemed to have no desire to make people stare, and being a man of good steady moral principles, as I thought, did not try to make theories out of what he had seen to confound virtue and vice . . . It was curious to see Cook, a grave steady man, and his wife, a decent plump Englishwoman, and think that he was preparing to sail round the world.

It would be good to know something more of the reality of the old woman who, left behind, lived well beyond her husband's time into a new age—an age that his discoveries did so much to shape.

EPILOGUE

The school of Cook

A number of the men who sailed with Cook went on to form a loose 'school' of exploration and scientific enquiry which was influential in the continued extension of geographical and ethnographical knowledge and the emergence of the modern scientific disciplines.

It would not be right to say that Cook was the 'master' of these men in every way. A number of them were accomplished in their own right before they became associated with him; and others most likely would have had notable careers even if they had not sailed with him. But voyaging the Pacific with the great explorer undoubtedly shaped their outlooks and encouraged them in methodical habits of investigation and record-keeping.

Here are some of those we may term members of 'Cook's school'.

Sir Joseph Banks (1743–1820)

Banks was one of the most extraordinary Europeans of the eighteenth century. As a youth, he developed a grand passion for botany, and used some of his large inheritance to have himself tutored in the subject according to the new Linnean precepts. As a young man, he ventured to Newfoundland; then, at his own expense, he sailed with a team of scientists and artists on the *Endeavour*. After that voyage, he went to Iceland. From 1778 until his death 42 years later, he presided over the affairs of the Royal Society, conducting a vast correspondence on a multitude of subjects with the learned of Europe and North America. He also advised the king and a succession of governments on such subjects as fen drainage, sheep breeding, agriculture, coinage, hemp cultivation and manufacture, exploration and colonisation. Banks sent a succession of young men to the ends of the earth to collect exotic or useful plants, insects and animals, which he then distributed to other areas—e.g., cochineal and bopal from Brazil to India; Chinese hemp to England and France; European culinary plants to Pacific islands; breadfruit from the Pacific to the West Indies. His role was similar to that of a modern scientific commission (e.g., the Australian CSIRO), but he played it largely single-handedly, and without payment.

Banks was influential in the Pitt administration's August 1786 decision to undertake a convict colonisation of New South Wales, and he interested himself in the colony's affairs until his death.

Joseph Billings (c. 1758–?)

Billings joined the *Discovery* as an able-bodied seaman, then transferred to the *Resolution* in September 1779. In 1783, he entered the Russian Navy as a midshipman; and in 1785, as 'the companion of Cook', the Empress Catherine appointed him to command an expedition intended to explore the northeastern coasts of Asia. On his way overland to Kamchatka to take up his command, Billings unexpectedly met his former shipmate John Ledyard at Yakutsk in Siberia. He conducted his explorations for a number of years thereafter. His subsequent fate is unknown.

William Bligh (1754–1817)

Bligh was master of the *Resolution* on Cook's third voyage. After making commercial voyages to the West Indies, he commanded the *Bounty* in 1787–89, on a trip to carry breadfruit from Tahiti to the West Indies. On 28 April 1789, a group of the crew led by Fletcher Christian mutinied, and cast Bligh and eighteen men adrift in an open boat with minimal food and equipment. Miraculously, Bligh reached Timor with the loss of only one man. In 1791–93, he made a second, successful, breadfruit voyage in the *Providence*.

Bligh held several commands between 1795 and 1802, including one under Nelson at the Battle of Copenhagen. In 1806, he arrived in Sydney as the newly appointed governor of the New South Wales colony. John Macarthur and a group of officers overthrew him on 26 January 1808. He spent two years in confinement, then returned to England, where he died in December 1817.

Bligh had too high an estimation of his own talents and was too demanding of those he considered his inferiors. Moreover, as the repeated rebellions against his authority show, he did not care how his violent language wounded other men's feelings. Danger and crisis brought out the best in him—a fact epitomised by his remarkable open-boat voyage.

James Colnett (1752?–1806)

Colnett joined the *Resolution* on Cook's second voyage as a midshipman. On his return, he served in a number of Royal Navy ships. Then, in 1786, the King George's Sound Company employed him to undertake a fur-trading voyage to the northwest Pacific coast. After collecting furs, then selling them in Macau, he had his ship seized at Nootka Sound by the Spanish commodore Martínez. When it was released he went back to Macau, then unsuccessfully attempted to breach the Japanese market.

Between 1793 and 1795, sailing in the privately owned *Rattler* but following Admiralty instructions, Colnett surveyed the southern Atlantic and Pacific Oceans on either side of South America, 'searching for Places . . . for Southern Whale Fisheries that voyaged round Cape Horn to refresh at'. He was promoted to Post-Captain in 1796; and in 1802–04, he took convicts on the *Glatton* to New South Wales, returning to England with a cargo of ship's timber.

Colnett's career encompassed many of the government and private initiatives taken to further Britain's imperial interests.

Georg Forster (1754–94)

Forster joined the *Resolution* on the second voyage as a scientist and assistant to his father, Johann. Much better tempered and accommodating than his father, Forster was particularly knowledgeable in botany and had a gift for languages. During the voyage, he and his father amassed extensive natural history collections.

After publishing *A Voyage round the World* (1777), Forster helped his father bring out *Observations made during a Voyage round the World* (1778), a pioneering attempt at understanding global wind and current systems, climate, and botanical and human distributions.

Having spent some time in Paris, Forster went to what is today Germany. In 1790, accompanied by the young scientist Alexander von Humboldt, whose intellectual development he influenced greatly, he revisited England. Caught up in the fervour of the French Revolution, he went to Paris again in 1793, where he died of pneumonia in January 1794.

Because he needed the money, Forster spent much of his energy on hack work. But in his thinking he was occasionally ahead of his time. In 1786, puzzling over the differences in human cultures he had observed in the Pacific, he asked (in C.J. Glacken's summary): 'Could not every region bring forth its own creatures adapted to its environment, and could not there be, by this reason, a multiple origin of mankind?'

John Gore (c. 1730–1790)

Gore was an American who some sources say was born in Virginia. He was master's mate on the *Dolphin* under both Byron (1764–66) and Wallis (1766–68). He then sailed as lieutenant under Cook on the *Endeavour*. Missing the second voyage when he accompanied Banks to Iceland, Gore sailed as first lieutenant on the *Resolution* on the third voyage, and assumed command of the expedition on 23 August 1779, after Charles Clerke's death. On his return, he was promoted to Post-Captain and appointed to Cook's position at Greenwich Hospital. Gore had an extraordinary life, for he circumnavigated the globe four times. And his description of the interior of Tahiti, published in Hawkesworth's *Voyages*, helped shape the popular image of that island into the twentieth century.

William Hodges (1744–97)

As artist on the *Resolution* on Cook's second voyage, Hodges made many drawings of Pacific peoples and watercolours that eloquently convey the ambience of this ocean's lush islands. After his return to England, he did a number of large oil paintings of Pacific scenes. His work from this period shows him grappling with the problems of how to represent water and air as constantly changing masses, and how to convey the nuances of light. He continued these interests when he travelled in India between 1778 and 1784, painting for Warren Hastings. Humboldt later said that it was Georg Forster's descriptions and Hodges's paintings that led him to develop 'an inextinguishable longing to visit the tropics'.

After failing as a banker, Hodges killed himself in 1797.

John Ledyard (1751–89)

Ledyard was an American, from Connecticut. He studied to be a minister, but after making a voyage to the Mediterranean, he joined the *Resolution* on the third voyage as corporal of marines. After his return to England, he deserted from British service rather than fight his countrymen in the American Revolutionary War, and then published his *Journal* of the circumnavigation (1783).

After the war, Ledyard tried to interest various parties, including Thomas Jefferson, in sponsoring a fur-trading voyage to the north-west Pacific coast. These proposals failing, he decided to travel overland to Kamchatka, take a Russian ship across to Nootka Sound, and then walk across North America to the east coast.

A powerfully built man who had unbounded confidence in his abilities but no money, Ledyard walked in the dead of winter around Scandinavia to St Petersburg, then took various forms of transport to Yakutsk, where he met Billings. Because he was making the trip against her express orders, the Empress Catherine had him arrested and deported to Poland.

Back in London, Banks asked Ledyard to go on an expedition in search of the Niger River. (Legend has it that when asked when he would be ready to leave, Ledyard replied: 'Tomorrow morning'.) In January 1789, before he could set out for the African interior, Ledyard died in Cairo of food poisoning and the medicine (vitriolic acid) he used to treat it.

Like Cook, Ledyard developed a modern sense of how being a true explorer involved stepping outside the bounds of one's own culture. He wrote memorably from Yakutsk:

> *& I will declare that I never was so totally at loss how to accommodate myself to my situation. The only consolation I have of the argumentative kind is to reflect . . . that to be travelling is to be in error; that this must more or less necessarily anticede the other, and that an error in judgement only, is always to be forgiven.*

James Matra (1746?–1806)

Matra (born James Magra) was the son of a wealthy New York doctor. He served in various ships during and after the Seven Years War (1756–63), then joined the *Endeavour* as a midshipman. Cook described him as 'one of those gentlemen, frequently found on board Kings Ships, that can very well be spared, or to speake more planer [arc] good for nothing'. Matra was most probably the author of the first published account of the voyage (1771).

In the mid-1770s, Matra was consul at Tenerife, in the Canary Islands. In order to claim a Corsican inheritance, he changed his name to Matra in 1776, but at the same time lost his American inheritance when the family supported the British in the War of Independence. After serving as secretary to the British embassy at Constantinople (1778–80), Matra returned to London, where he tried to interest politicians in a series of imperial schemes, including the colonisation of New South Wales.

When the government did adopt this idea in 1786, but declined to appoint Matra governor, Banks got him the position of consul at Tangier in Morocco. He never saw England (or America) again.

Matra had a keen interest in other cultures, and his letters to the Home Office and to Banks vividly describe Morocco before it became a European colony. He also enquired into the geography of the interior of Africa and assisted travellers sent by the Africa Association.

Edward Riou (1758?–1801)

Riou joined the *Discovery* on the third voyage as a midshipman, transferring to the *Resolution* in September 1779. He saw service in home waters, at Newfoundland, and in the West Indies. In 1789, he was appointed to take the *Guardian*, laden with stores and plants, and carrying agricultural supervisors and convict artificers, to the struggling colony at Sydney. But 2000 kilometres out from Cape Town, and within six weeks of Sydney, the *Guardian* struck an iceberg. About half the complement abandoned a ship they thought would surely sink within hours. For the next eight weeks, the rudderless, waterlogged ship veered crazily about the southern Indian Ocean, yet amazingly Riou and the remaining crew managed to get it back to Cape Town. It was a feat of navigation to rival Bligh's, and one observer wrote how he was 'struck by the singular energy of Captn Riou's figure, when he brought the *Guardian* to anchor in Table Bay'.

After Riou was killed in the Battle of Copenhagen, Lord Nelson wrote: 'In poor dear Riou the country has sustained an irreparable loss.'

George Vancouver (1759–98)

Vancouver joined the *Resolution* on the second voyage as a midshipman. Legend has it that as Cook gave the order to turn about from

71°10'S latitude, Vancouver ran to the bowsprit and cried, '*Ne plus ultra!*'—i.e., 'no one has gone further [south]'. He then sailed as midshipman on the *Discovery* on the third voyage.

Promoted to lieutenant in 1780, Vancouver served in the West Indies between 1781 and 1789. Early in 1791, he took command of two ships to accept restitution of Nootka Sound from the Spanish and to survey the American coastline for the supposed Northwest Passage. For three summers, Vancouver worked on his surveys, which in some ways were even more rigorous and precise than those of Cook. Indeed, this voyage marks the transition between the great eighteenth-century oceanic explorations, as exemplified by Cook's, and the painstaking, extended nineteenth-century surveys such as those by the *Beagle* and the *Rattlesnake*.

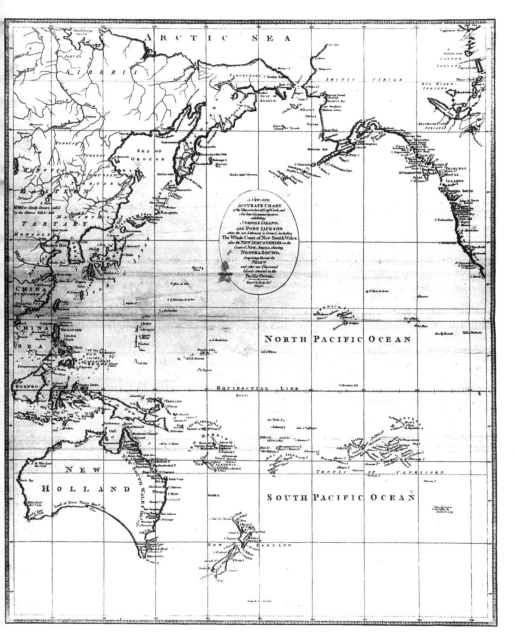

[Anon.], An New and Accurate Chart of the Discoveries of Capn Cook and other later Circumnavigators.

BIBLIOGRAPHY

My account of eighteenth-century Pacific exploration is based on five kinds of sources: unpublished letters and journals, mostly in the Public Record Office, British Library, and National Maritime Museum, London; contemporary narratives of the voyages; modern editions of the explorers' journals and letters; modern catalogues of the charts and drawings made during the voyages;  and modern historical studies. Quotations from unpublished materials appear by kind permission of the Controller of Her Majesty's Stationery Office, the British Library Board, and the Director, National Maritime Museum. Contemporary narratives are listed in the first section of the bibliography, and modern editions of primary written sources in the second. Catalogues of the artists' works are listed in the third section. There is now a vast literature dealing with Captain James Cook and the European exploration of the Pacific Ocean. For the benefit of readers who may be interested in finding out more about particular topics, in the fourth section of the bibliography I have listed a selection of the more reliable and/or up-to-date studies.

1 Contemporary narratives

Anson

Walter, Richard and Robins, Benjamin, *A Voyage round the World by George Anson*, ed. Glyndwr Williams, Oxford University Press, London, 1974.

Baudin

Péron, François Auguste, *A Voyage of Discovery to the Southern Hemisphere*, London, 1809.
——and Louis Claude Desaules de Freycinet, *Voyage de découvertes aux terres Australes*, 2 vols, Paris, 1807–16.

Bligh

Bligh, William, *A Voyage to the South Sea*, London, 1792.

Bougainville

Bougainville, Louis Antoine de, *Voyage autour du monde*, Paris, 1771.
——*A Voyage round the World*, trans. J.R. Forster, London, 1772.

Campbell

Campbell, John, *Navigantium atque Itinerantium Bibliotheca*, 2 vols, London, 1744–48.

Cook

Cook, James, *A Voyage towards the South Pole*, 2 vols, London, 1777.
——and James King, *A Voyage to the Pacific Ocean*, 3 vols, London, 1784.
Forster, Georg, *A Voyage round the World*, 2 vols, London, 1777.
Forster, John Reinhold, *Observations made during a Voyage round the World*, London, 1778.
Hawkesworth, John, comp. , *An Account of the Voyages undertaken . . . for making Discoveries in the Southern Hemisphere, and successively performed by Commodore Byron, Captain Wallis, Captain Carteret, and Captain Cook*, 3 vols, London, 1773.
Parkinson, Sydney, *A Journal of a Voyage to the South Seas*, London, 1773.
Samwell, David, *A Narrative of the Death of Captain James Cook*, London, 1786.

Entrecasteaux

Labillardière, Jacques Julien Houton de, *Relation du voyage à la recherche de la Pérouse*, 2 vols, Paris, 1799.
——*Voyage in Search of La Pérouse*, London, 1800.

Flinders

Flinders, Matthew, *A Voyage to Terra Australis*, 3 vols, London, 1814.

Lapérouse

Lapérouse, Jean-François de Galaup, de, *Voyage de la Pérouse autour du monde*, ed. L.A. Milet-Mureau, 2 vols, Paris, 1797.

——*A Voyage round the World*, 2 vols, London, 1799.

Vancouver
Vancouver, George, *A Voyage of Discovery to the North Pacific Ocean*, 3 vols, London, 1798.

2 Published sources

Banks
The Endeavour *Journal of Joseph Banks, 1768–1771*, ed. J.C. Beaglehole, 2nd ed., 2 vols, Trustees of the Public Library of New South Wales in association with Angus & Robertson, Sydney, 1963.

Baudin
The Journal of Post Captain Nicolas Baudin, trans. and ed. Christine Cornell, Libraries Board of South Australia, Adelaide, 1974.

Bligh
Return to Tahiti: Bligh's Second Breadfruit Voyage, ed. Douglas Oliver, Melbourne University Press, Melbourne, 1988.

Bougainville
Bougainville et ses Compagnons autour du Monde, 1766–1769, ed. E. Taillemite, 2 vols, Imprimerie Nationale, Paris, 1977.
Anonymous, *News from New Cythera: A Report of Bougainville's Voyage, 1766–1769*, ed. L.D. Hammond, University of Minnesota Press, Minneapolis, 1970.

Burney
The Private Journal of James Burney, ed. Beverley Hooper, National Library of Australia, Canberra, 1975.

Byron
Byron's Journal of his Circumnavigation 1764–1766, ed. R.E. Gallagher, Hakluyt Society, Cambridge, 1964.

Carteret
Carteret's Voyage round the World, 1766–1769, ed. Helen Wallis, 2 vols, Hakluyt Society, Cambridge, 1965.

Cook

The Journals of Captain James Cook on his Voyages of Discovery, ed. J.C. Beaglehole, 3 vols, Hakluyt Society, London, 1955–67.

Elliott, John, and Pickersgill, Richard, *Captain Cook's Second Voyage*, ed. Christine Holmes, Caliban Books, London, 1984.

Lapérouse

Le Voyage de Lapérouse, ed. John Dunmore and Maurice de Brossard, 2 vols, Imprimerie Nationale, Paris, 1985.

The Journal of Jean-François de Galaup de la Pérouse 1785–1788, trans. and ed. John Dunmore, 2 vols, Hakluyt Society, London, 1994–95.

Malaspina

Catalogo Critico de los Documentos de la Expedicion Malaspina (1789–1794) del Museo Naval, ed. D. Higueras Rodriguez, Museo Naval, Madrid, n.d.

Surville

Surville, Jean de and Labé, Guillaume, *The Expedition of the St Jean-Baptiste to the Pacific, 1769–1770*, trans. and ed. John Dunmore, Hakluyt Society, London, 1981.

Vancouver

Vancouver, George, *A Voyage of Discovery to the North Pacific Ocean*, ed. W. Kaye Lamb, 4 vols, Hakluyt Society, London, 1984.

Wallis

Robertson, George, *The Discovery of Tahiti*, ed. Hugh Carrington, Hakluyt Society, London, 1948.

3 Art and charts

Baudin

Baudin in Australian Waters: The Artwork of the French Voyage of Discovery to the Southern Lands, 1800–1804, eds Elliot Forsyth, et al., Oxford University Press, Melbourne, 1988.

Cook

The Art of Captain Cook's Voyages, eds Rüdiger Joppien and Bernard Smith, 4 vols, Oxford University Press, Melbourne, 1984–87.

The Charts & Coastal Views of Captain Cook's Voyages, eds Andrew David, et al., Hakluyt Society, London, 1988– .

Flinders

Drawings by William Westall: Landscape Artist on Board H.M.S. Investigator During the Circumnavigation of Australia by Captain Matthew Flinders R.N. in 1801–1803, eds T.M. Perry and D.H. Simpson, Royal Commonwealth Society, London, 1962.

Malaspina

Catalogo de los Dibujos Aguadas y Acuarelas de la Expedicion Malaspina, ed. Mercedes Palau de Inglesias, Museo de America, Madrid, 1980.

Enlightened Voyages: Malaspina and Galiano on the Northwest Coast, eds. John Kendrick and Robin Inglis, Vancouver Maritime Museum, Vancouver, 1991.

4 Modern historical studies

Amalric, Pierre, ed., *Bicentenaire du Voyage de Lapérouse*, Association Lapérouse, Albi, 1985.

Bartroli, Tomas, *Brief Presence: Spain's Activity on America's Northwest Coast (1774–1796)*, Tomas Bartroli, Vancouver, 1991.

Baugh, Daniel, *Naval Administration in the Age of Walpole*, Princeton University Press, Princeton, 1965.

Beaglehole, J. C., *The Exploration of the Pacific*, 3rd ed., Stanford University Press, Stanford, 1966.

——*The Life of Captain James Cook*, Adam & Charles Black, London, 1974.

Bray, R. J. 'Australia and the transit of Venus', CSIRO Information Service, Sheet No. 1–35, February 1981.

Cook, Warren L., *Flood Tide of Empire: Spain and the Pacific Northwest, 1543–1819*, Yale University Press, New Haven, Conn., 1973. (The analysis of the purposes of Malaspina's expedition quoted on p. 77 appears on p. 118 of this book.)

David, Andrew, *The Artists of Vancouver's Voyage to the Northwest Coast of*

America, Vancouver Conference on Exploration and Discovery, Vancouver, 1991.

Dening, Greg, *Islands and Beaches: Discourse on a Silent Land: Marquesas, 1774–1880,* Melbourne University Press, Melbourne, 1980.

——'Sharks that walk on the land: The death of Captain Cook', *Meanjin,* 41, 1982, 427–37.

——*Mr Bligh's Bad Language: Passion, Power and Theatre on the Bounty,* Cambridge University Press, New York, 1992. (My account of the *Dolphin's* arrival at Tahiti is based on Dening's, from whom I have also taken the terms 'Native' and 'Stranger'.)

Dunmore, John, *French Explorers in the Pacific,* 2 vols, Clarendon Press, Oxford, 1965–69.

——*Pacific Explorer: The Life of Jean-François de La Pérouse,* Dunmore Press, Palmerston North, 1985.

Duyker, Edward, *An Officer of the Blue: Marc-Joseph Marion Dufresne, South Sea Explorer, 1724–1772,* Melbourne University Press, Melbourne, 1994.

Fisher, Robin and Johnston, Hugh, eds, *Captain James Cook and his Times,* Douglas and McIntyre, Vancouver, 1979.

——*From Maps to Metaphors: The Pacific World of George Vancouver,* University of British Columbia Press, Vancouver, 1993.

Frost, Alan, *Convicts and Empire: A Naval Question, 1776–1811,* Oxford University Press, Melbourne, 1980.

——*The Precarious Life of James Mario Matra,* Melbourne University Press, Melbourne, 1995.

——*Arthur Phillip, 1738–1814: His Voyaging,* Oxford University Press, Melbourne, 1987.

——*Botany Bay Mirages: Illusions of Australia's Convict Beginnings,* Melbourne University Press, Melbourne, 1994.

Gaziello, Catherine, *L'Expédition de Lapérouse, 1785–1788: Réplique française aux voyages de Cook,* C.T.H.S., Paris, 1984.

Glacken, C. J., *Traces on the Rhodian Shore: Nature and Culture in Western Thought from Ancient Times to the End of the Eighteenth Century,* Berkeley, University of California Press, 1967.

Hardy, John and Frost, Alan, eds, *European Voyaging towards Australia,* Australian Academy of the Humanities, Canberra, 1990.

Harlow, V.T., *The Founding of the Second British Empire, 1763–1793,* 2 vols, Longmans Green, London, 1952, 1964.

Horner, Frank, *The French Reconnaissance: Baudin in Australia, 1801–1803,* Melbourne University Press, 1987.

——*Looking for La Pérouse: D'Entrecasteaux in Australia and the South Pacific, 1792–1793*, Melbourne University Press, Melbourne, 1995.

Howe, Kerry, *Where the Waves Fall: A New South Sea Islands History from First Settlement to Colonial Rule*, George Allen & Unwin, Sydney, 1984.

Inglis, Robin, ed., *Spain and the North Pacific Coast*, Vancouver Maritime Museum, Vancouver, 1992.

King, Robert J. *The Secret History of the Convict Colony: Alexandro Malaspina's report on the British settlement of New South Wales*, Allen & Unwin, Sydney, 1990.

Mackay, David, *In the Wake of Cook: Exploration, Science & Empire, 1780–1801*, Victoria University Press, Wellington, 1985.

Marshall, P. J. and Williams, Glyndwr, *The Great Map of Mankind: British Perceptions of the World in the Age of Enlightenment*, Dent, London, 1982.

Palau de Inglesias, Mercedes, ed., *La Expedicion Malaspina, 1789–1794*, Ministro de Cultura, Madrid, 1984.

Plomley, N. J. B., *The Baudin Expedition and the Tasmanian Aborigines, 1802*, Blubber Head Press, Hobart, 1983.

Richard, Hélène, *Le voyage de d'Entrecasteaux à la recherche de Lapérouse*, C.T.H.S., Paris, 1986.

Rodger, N. A. M., *The Wooden World: An Anatomy of the Georgian Navy*, Annapolis, Naval Institute Press, 1986.

Sahlins, Marshall, *Historical Metaphors and Mythical Realities: Structure in the Early History of the Sandwich Islands Kingdom*, University of Michigan Press, Ann Arbor, 1981.

Salmond, Anne, *Two Worlds: First Meetings between Maori and Europeans, 1642–1772*, Viking, Auckland, 1991.

Shaw, Carlos M., ed., *El Pacifico Español de Magallanes a Malaspina*, Ministerio de Asuntos Exteriores, Madrid, 1988.

Smith, Bernard, *European Vision and the South Pacific*, 2nd ed., Yale University Press, New Haven, Conn., 1984.

——*Imagining the Pacific: In the Wake of the Cook Voyages*, Melbourne University Press, Melbourne, 1992.

Spate, O.H.K., *The Pacific Since Magellan*, 3 vols, Australian National University Press, Canberra, 1979–88.

Tovell, Freeman, *Bodega y Quadra returns to the Americas*, Vancouver Conference on Exploration and Discovery, Vancouver, 1990.

Williams, Glyndwr, ' "Far more happier than we Europeans": Reactions to the Australian Aborigines on Cook's voyage', *Australian Historical Studies*, 19, 1981, pp. 499–512.

——The British Search for the Northwest Passage in the Eighteenth Century, Longmans, London, 1962.

Withey, Lynne, Voyages of Discovery: Captain Cook and the Exploration of the Pacific, University of California Press, Berkeley and Los Angeles, 1987.

INDEX